M000214654

THE

Community

OF THOSE

WHO

HAVE

NOTHING

IN COMMON

Studies in Continental Thought
John Sallis, general editor

Consulting Editors

Robert Bernasconi   William L. McBride
Rudolf Bernet   J. N. Mohanty
John D. Caputo   Mary Rawlinson
David Carr   Tom Rockmore
Edward S. Casey   Calvin O. Schrag
Hubert L. Dreyfus   Reiner Schürmann
Don Ihde   Charles E. Scott
David Farrell Krell   Thomas Sheehan
Lenore Langsdorf   Robert Sokolowski
Alphonso Lingis   Bruce W. Wilshire
David Wood

ALPHONSO LINGIS

THE

Community

OF THOSE

WHO

HAVE

NOTHING

IN COMMON

INDIANA UNIVERSITY PRESS
Bloomington and Indianapolis

© 1994 by Alphonso Lingis
All rights reserved

No part of this book may be reproduced or utilized in any
form or by any means, electronic or mechanical, including
photocopying and recording, or by any information storage
and retrieval system, without permission in writing from
the publisher. The Association of American University
Presses' Resolution on Permissions constitutes the only
exception to this prohibition.

The paper used in this publication meets the minimum
requirements of American National Standard for
Information Sciences—Permanence of Paper for Printed
Library Materials, ANSI Z39.48-1984.

Manufactured in the United States of America

Library of Congress Cataloging-in-Publication Data

Lingis, Alphonso, date
    The community of those who have nothing in
common / Alphonso Lingis.
        p.   cm. — (Studies in Continental thought)
        ISBN 0-253-33438-1 (alk. paper). —
        ISBN 0-253-20852-1 (pbk. : alk. paper)
        1. Man. 2. Reason. 3. Death.   I. Title. II. Series.
B945.L4583C66   1994
179'.7—dc20   93-23955

    2 3 4 5   99 98

CONTENTS

$\mathcal{C}$ommunity is usually conceived as constituted by a number of individuals having something in common— a common language, a common conceptual frame- work—and building something in common: a nation, a polis, an institution. I started to think of those who are leaving everything—who are dying. Death comes singularly for each; each one dies alone, Heidegger said. But, in hospitals, I had many hours to think of the necessity, among the living, to accompany those who are dying. Not only is this true of the doctors and nurses, who do all they can, but of the one who goes to stay with the dying one to the end and who stays when there is no longer any healing possible—who knows in his or her heart he or she has to stay. It is the hardest thing there is, but one knows it is what one has to do. Not only because it is a parent or lover who is dying, someone with whom one has lived one's life; one will stay when, in the next bed or the next room, there is someone one never knew, dying alone.

Is this the critical point of individual morality only? I came to think that a society that would forsake the dying to die alone, whether in hospitals or in the gutters, undermines itself radically.

Is there not a growing conviction, clearer today among innumerable people, that the dying of people with whom we have nothing in common—no racial kinship, no language, no religion, no economic interests—concerns us? We obscurely feel that our generation is being judged, ultimately, by the abandon of the Cambodians, and Somalians, and the social outcasts in the streets of our own cities.

Coming back from these thoughts, I came to understand that what concerns us in another is precisely his or her otherness—which appeals to us and contests us when he faces. The essay "The Intruder" circumscribes this otherness. The essay "Faces, Idols, Fetishes" explains how real values are not what we have in common, but what individualizes each one and makes him or her other. In "The Murmur of the World," I set out to show that language is not simply a code established by convention among humans, that levels our experiences such that they can be treated as equivalent and interchangeable, but that human language has to be seen as arising out of the murmur of nature—of animals and finally of all things that are and that resound. In the sonority of our codes we communicate not only with human decoders, but with the chant and the complaint and the cacophony of nature. "The Elemental That Faces" studies the situation where what is said is inessential; what is essential is that I be there and speak. "Carrion Body Carrion Utterance" is concerned with torture, which arises in a specific linguistic situation: the victim is being forced to say that all that he or she said and believed is lies, that he or she is incapable of truth. Finally, "Community in Death " addresses the community one has with the dying.

the other community

*f*rom the beginning, philosophical thought, unlike the wisdom of the sages of pre-Socratic Greece, India, Persia, and China, was linked to the cause of building community. The rational form of knowledge produces a common discourse that is integrally one and a new kind of community, a community, in principle, unlimited.

Rational science is not distinguishable from the empirical knowledge of the great sedentary civilizations of India, China, the Mayas, the Incas, or from that of the nomads who have survived for centuries in their often harsh environments, by its content of observations. Claude Lévi-Strauss, in *The Savage Mind*, showed that the Amazonian Americans had elaborated a representation of their environment that was rigorously empirical. Their procedures scrupulously distinguished effective knowledge from hearsay and approximation. Their identification of the species, properties, and uses of the natural substances and living things of their environment was often far more comprehensive than that now contained in the data of our botany, zoology, and pharmaceutical science.

Their representations were equivalent to ours in the exigency for empirical rigor in observation and verification; its realization was limited only by the limits of the region to which they had cognitive access and by the technological limits of their tools for exploring and experimenting. Nor were their bodies of knowledge inferior to our botany, zoology, geology, meteorology, and astronomy in the intrinsic coherence and consistency of their patterns of organization.

What the West calls science is not accumulations of observations but explanatory systems. Edmund Husserl defined the rational will which engendered science and philosophy as the will to give a reason. Reasons are products of thought, and rational knowledge presents itself not as the sum-total of impressions left on individuals by the action of alien forces, but as a constructive work. In what the West calls science, for every batch of observations recorded and sorted, thought seeks to produce a reason. The reason is a more general formulation from which the observations could be deduced. It is what we call an empirical law. Then thought seeks to give a reason for the reason. This is what we call a theory, from which empirical laws could be deduced. Thought seeks to create a theory of all the theories in every branch of scientific research, the Standard Model from which, in high-energy particle physics, the theories of quantum mechanics, radioactivity, and electromagnetism could be derived. Rational science is, Werner Heisenberg wrote, bent on "being able to write one single fundamental equation from which the properties of all elementary particles, and therewith the behavior of all matter whatever follow." Philosophy seeks to give reasons for the rational procedures, elaborates theories of the relationship between rational thought and reality, seeks reasons to believe in rational thought.

The will to give a reason characterizes a certain discursive practice. In the mercantile port cities of Greece, strangers arrive who ask the Greeks, Why do you do as you do? In all societies where groups of humans elaborate their distinctness, the answer was and is, Because our fathers have taught us to do so, because our gods have decreed that it be so. Something new begins when the Greeks begin to give a reason that the stranger, who does not have these fathers and these gods, can accept, a reason that any lucid mind can accept. Such speech acts are pledges. The one who so answers commits himself to his statement, commits himself to supply a reason and a reason for the reason; he makes himself responsible for his statement. He commits himself to answer for what he says to every contestation. He accepts every stranger as his judge.

Rational practice elaborates a discourse that is one and common to any lucid mind. In what each one says on his own and takes responsibility for, he finds implicated what the others say. The whole system of rational discourse is implicated in the statements put forth by any researcher, by anyone who endeavors to think rationally. Each one speaks as a representative of the common discourse. His own insights and utterances become part of the anonymous discourse of universal reason.

This discursive practice then invokes a human community in principle unlimited. A community in which each one, in facing the other, faces an imperative that he formulate all his encounters and insights in universal terms, in forms that could be the information belonging to everyone. — People make their opinions the answers to everything.

The discourse that, to the stranger who asks, Why do you do as you do?, answers, Because our fathers have taught us to do so, because our gods have decreed that it be so, elaborates the distinctness of the multitude who speak thus. Moreover, this discourse is not internally one, as is rational discourse. Among the statements that formulate impressions left on individuals by the action of alien forces, there are a multiplicity of dicta, of ancestors or divinities, that recur in the speech as passwords of an autochthonous multitude. Actions determined by the dicta of ancestors or divinities can well enlist, in communal works or monuments, all those who trace their birth and their place to them, but such works elaborate the distinctness of a progeny or a chosen race. discussion/debate/thought

The production of rational discourse transforms action. Actions driven by mute drives and cravings of

Peoples normal desires and then shaped by their ancestral customs, and therefore are not their own.

attach reasons to desires

one's own are transformed into actions motivated by reasons, which, as reasons, are not one's own, and solicit the assent of others. Such initiatives can enlist the efforts of others in common motivations and become collective actions. Each one invests his or her forces and passion in enterprises that absorb and depersonalize him and her and that endure and go on working or disintegrate without him or her. When we view enterprises in the public field, our own or those of others, we explain them with reasons which belong to no one and to everyone.

collective identities make us less individualized

We rationalists perceive the reality of being members of a community in the reality of works undertaken and realized; we perceive the community itself as a work. The rationality of our discourse lies in the reasons adduced and produced; we perceive reason as a work—an enterprise and an achievement. The rational discourse we produce materializes in collective enterprises. To build community would mean to collaborate in industry which organizes the division of labor and to participate in the market. It would mean to participate in the elaboration of a political structure, laws and command posts. It would be to collaborate with others to build up public works and communications.

how we think that reason = enterprise

build community → unity = labor market public works → practical reasonings

Wherever we find works that are collective enterprises we find thought of which our own (that is, the thought we make our own by answering for it on our own, making it rational) is a representative. In the public works and monuments of North America we see inscribed the motivations and goals of us North Americans; in our factories, airports, and highways we see our reasoned choices among our needs and wants, and our plans. In our system of laws and our social institutions, we recognize our formulated experience, our judgment, our debated consensuses. In our rational collective enterprises, we find, in principle, nothing alien to us, foreign, and impervious to our understanding; we find only ourselves. We do not, like the Balinese, find in our institutions, public works, and community gatherings the visitation of alien spirits, demonic and divine forces, or pacts made with the forces of volcanoes and rivers and skies. We find, behind the signs attributed to men's gods, reasons in common human psychological needs and drives.

In the thought of the Amazonian Indians or of nomadic Maasai who wander the Rift Valley in East Africa where human primates have wandered for four million years without leaving any construction, we can recognize only the memory of impressions left by alien forces on multiplicities of individual minds alien to us. We see the evidence for a community, and the signs that a community existed in the past, in roads, aqueducts, ports, temples, and monuments. We enter into that community by constructing the reasons that motivated its constructions. In the Great Wall of China, the Inca roads cut in the Andes, the pyramids built in Egypt and Central America, the irrigation system of Angkor, we find thought at work of which our own is a representative. Our economics, political science, ecological science, psychology, and psychoanalysis supply, behind the dicta taken to be of ancestors or divinities which ordered these collective works, reasons which motivated them. They cease to be constructions that materialized the distinctness of a progeny or a chosen race. Elaborating reasons behind the dicta they took to be of ancestors or divinities that ordered the construction of these collective works, we find we have elaborated reasons to conserve or reconstruct them. We thus enlist, and enlist the Chinese, Aztecs, and Khmer, albeit posthumously, in universal humanity.

We see the evidence for our community in the animals, vegetables, and minerals of our environment. We enter into that community by understanding our material environment, reconstructing the reasons that motivated its production.

For the environment in which our community subsists is one it produces. It is not a thing's own nature, its properties linking it with its natural setting, that makes it useful to us, but the properties it reveals when inserted into the instrumental system we have laid out. Rational practice makes the practicable field about us the common field of collective enterprises. Timber is first cut into rectangular boards before it can be useful; the trees themselves are first hybridized, thinned out, and pruned before they can become useful as timber. It is not willow bark in its nature as willow bark that we find useful for our headaches, but the extracted and purified essence synthesized into aspirin tablets. There are whole plantations now where biologically engineered species of plants grow not on the earth but in water, anchored on floats of plastic foam fed by chemical blends. There are reserves now where genetic engineering is producing new species of patented plants and animals. Our research laboratories do not study natural entities, but instead study pure water, pure sulfur, and pure uranium which are found nowhere in nature and which are produced in the laboratory. The table of elements itself is no longer an inventory of irreducible physical nature; atomic fission and fusion makes them all subject to transformation. The community which produces, and is produced by, reasons produces the means of its subsistence and the material of its knowledge.

As a biological species, we are ourselves man-made; our specific biological traits—our enormously enlarged neocortex, the complexity of our bodies' neural organization, the expanded representation of the thumb on our cortex, our upright posture, and our hairlessness—did not evolve naturally to differentiate us from the other primates, but evolved as a result of our invention of symbolic systems, evolved from feedback from culture—the perfecting of tools, the organization of hunting and gathering, the establishing of families, the control of fire, and especially the reliance on systems of significant symbols—language, ritual, and art—for orientation, communication, and self-control. These systems of significant symbols delineate the distinctness of the multitude who use them; our specific biological traits materialize this distinctness as the distinctness of a progeny. The rational elaboration of significant symbols transforms our biological specificity, making our species one composed of individuals representative of a universal community.

True. Our physical construction shapes very basically who we are.

Rational discourse and practice makes nature a communal work and makes our own nature our own work. We civilized men who have produced our own environment see on everything in it the form and shape and species given to the raw material of nature by collective human intentions and effort, which are produced by the practice of rational discourse. The man-made species we are, which produces its own nature in an environment it produces, finds nothing within itself that is alien to itself, opaque and impervious to its own understanding. The individual of modern culture, who affirms himself with his inalienable rights and sets himself up as legislator of his own laws, sets out to produce his individuality as that of a nature closed upon itself. In the human community

repeated

We see nothing weird abt ourselves b/c we see what we do as right. We don't see ourselves as just another species w/ its own traits.

he finds a work closed in itself and representative of his own thought. As the individual finds that his own thought is representative of the whole system of rational thought, he will find on his fellow-man but the reflection of his own rational nature.

Before the rational community, there was the encounter with the other, the intruder. The encounter begins with the one who exposes himself to the demands and contestation of the other. Beneath the rational community, its common discourse of which each lucid mind is but the representative and its enterprises in which the efforts and passions of each are absorbed and depersonalized, is another community, the community that demands that the one who has his own communal identity, who produces his own nature, expose himself to the one with whom he has nothing in common, the stranger.

This *other community* is not simply absorbed into the rational community; it recurs, it troubles the rational community, as its double or its shadow.

This *other community* forms not in a work, but in the interruption of work and enterprises. It is not realized in having or in producing something in common but in exposing oneself to the one with whom one has nothing in common: to the Aztec, the nomad, the guerrilla, the enemy. The other community forms when one recognizes, in the face of the other, an imperative. An imperative that not only contests the

+ we are so disturbed by our differences
that we don't pay attention to our similarities.

common discourse and community from which he or she is excluded, but everything one has or sets out to build in common with him or her.

It is not only with one's rational intelligence that one exposes oneself to an imperative. Our rational intelligence cannot arise without commanding our sensibility, which must collect data from the environment in comprehensible and regular ways, commanding our motor powers to measure the forces, obstacles, and causalities of the practicable field in comprehensible and regular ways, and commanding our sensibility to others to register the relations of command and obedience at work in the social field in comprehensible and regular ways. It is with the nakedness of one's eyes that one exposes oneself to the other, with one's hands arrested in their grip on things and turned now to the other, open-handed, and with the disarmed frailty of one's voice troubled with the voice of another.

One exposes oneself to the other—the stranger, the destitute one, the judge—not only with one's insights and one's ideas, that they may be contested, but one also exposes the nakedness of one's eyes, one's voice and one's silences, one's empty hands. For the other, the stranger, turns to one, not only with his or her convictions and judgments, but also with his or her frailty, susceptibility, mortality. He or she turns to one his or her face, idol and fetish. He or she turns to one a face made of carbon compounds, dust that shall

Being criticized
is not just all
one's accepted
culture + beliefs
+ morals, but
also one's sense
of self. If
one's God is
questioned, one's
existence and
purpose is
questioned.

return to dust, a face made of earth and air, made of warmth, of blood, made of light and shadow. He or she turns to one flesh scarred and wrinkled with suffering and with mortality. Community forms when one exposes oneself to the naked one, the destitute one, the outcast, the dying one. One enters into community not by affirming oneself and one's forces but by exposing oneself to expenditure at a loss, to sacrifice. Community forms in a movement by which one exposes oneself to the other, to forces and powers outside oneself, to death and to the others who die.

The rational community that forms in the exchange of information exchanges abstract entities, idealized signs of idealized referents. Communication is extracting the message from irrelevant and conflicting signals—noise. Interlocutors are allied in a struggle against noise; the ideal city of communication would be maximally purged of noise. But there is noise internal to the message—the opacity of the voice that transmits it. And there is the background noise of the world which cannot be silenced without silencing our voices too. By envisioning the human voice in the perspective of evolutionary biology, we learn to hear the murmur of the world, which human voices continue and make resound for one another.

Beyond the communication with one another through signals, abstract entities, in the community allied against the rumble of the world, we make contact with inhuman things by embracing their forms and

We take characteristics/dispositions/beliefs from each other, as well as give

their matter. We also make contact with one another by contracting another's form, by transubstantiating our own material state.

excluding

The community that produces something in common, that establishes truth and that now establishes a technological universe of simulacra, excludes the savages, the mystics, the psychotics—excludes their utterances and their bodies. It excludes them in its own space: tortures.

making/doubt

~ making

(?)

on killing/ destroying "the real world"

In the midst of the work of the rational community, there forms the community of those who have nothing in common, of those who have nothingness, death, their mortality, in common. But is the death that isolates each one a common death? And can it be identified as nothingness?

everyone dies

Is every death the same?
Is death nothingness?

—

clearly explained

Kant isolated and elucidated the imperative to give a reason which the rational subject obeys. This imperative is not simply an order observed outside, in the practice of a certain kind of society. The rational subject obeys an imperative that, Kant set out to show, weighs immediately on the mind of the individual. The rational community takes form as a result of this prior subjection to an imperative which each thoughtful subject discovers in himself.

People realize the imperative as valid

Kant conceived the rational community as a republic of autonomous agents, each obeying the order that commands the others by obeying the order he legislates for himself. But when we examine how, in Kant's analysis, the rational agent encounters the other, we find that the figure of the other, rationally comprehended, doubles up into an image of sensuous suffering and mortality. In this double visage of the other, we can see a double contact with him and a double community taking form.

universal law

no idea

Thought, conceptual thought, is the practice of conceiving for sensory patterns we perceive; for the masses, forces, and resistances we manipulate; for the looks, vocalizations, and gestures of others, consistent and coherent conceptual terms. Rational thought is the practice of formulating, for observations, the laws of nature, formulating, for actions and operations, technical rules, and formulating, for encounters with others, the order of society. Thought represents the shifting sensory patterns of our environment with consistent and coherent empirical concepts and represents the environment as a whole comprehensively with the laws of nature. Thought represents the forces and resistances of the field about us with the means-end order of practicable reality. Thought represents the looks, voices, and gestures of others about the thinker with the economic, juridic, and political rules of the social order.

As soon as thought arises, it finds itself subject to an imperative. In order to recognize something in the passing patterns of the spectacle about one, one *has to* form correct concepts. In order to recognize constellations of patterns one *has to* reason rightly. The imperative that weighs on thought is a fact. It is the first fact; empirical facts can be encountered as facts only by a thought that is bound to conceive them correctly.

Thought can form inconsistent concepts and can reason incoherently. Thought finds itself not determined to conceive correctly and reason rightly, but

Thought doesn't always want to find the right answer; another, lesser answer is usually good enough.

obligated to do so. Thought, the activity of compre-
hending sensory impressions with concepts and of organizing concepts, does not arise as a drive in our nature or as a free initiative. An imperative weighs on
thought; <u>thought finds itself commanded to think.</u>
<u>Thought is obedience.</u>

thought comes from feelings that develop concepts on what we feel. It isn't in our nature. We think ble we feel we must think. — It keeps us in line.

We collect impressions by exposing our sensory
surfaces to the things about us, by moving over the
solid surfaces and against the obstacles about us, ma-
neuvering with and manipulating their forces, and by
interacting with other sentient and self-moving
agents. In order to comprehend the passing patterns
as consistent units and to recognize constellations of
units that recur, one has to be able to command one's
sensory organs to collect sensory perceptions in ordered ways, one has to be able to command one's
posture and the forces in one's limbs, and one has to
be <u>able to command the moves with which one's</u>
<u>body</u> exposes itself to others and faces them.
<u>Thought, which finds itself commanded to think, finds</u>
<u>itself commanded to be in command.</u> Thought must
command its sensory-motor faculties so as to collect
impressions that it can comprehend with requisite
concepts and relate with cogent reasons. Thought
must produce representations that function as commands that program the sensibility of the body, its
movements among things, and its postures before
others.

commands

— Thought makes us want to make sense out of what we feel & perceive.

We do not have, Kant accepted from Hume, any perception of causality; we do not have any perception of the causality of our representations to order our will and the nervous circuitry and musculature of our bodies. But we have to think—we are commanded by the imperative that weighs on our thought to think—that they can so order them.

And we sense that they can. There is, in the receptivity of our sensitive surfaces, a feeling of being not only informed by the forms but affected by the forces of our environment; this feeling is the pleasure and the pain with which we perceive them. There is also, in the initiatives by which our thought arises over those impressions to identify them and to relate them, a feeling of being subjected to the weight of the imperative. Kant identifies this sense of finding oneself, in the very spontaneity of one's thought that forms concepts and relates them, burdened with the force of the imperative, the sentiment of respect.

The sentiment of respect is, Kant says, something like inclination, something like fear—like the pain in fear. This pain is not the sense of constriction felt by our sensuous faculties under the force of a foreign material object that presses into our substance and wounds it. It is the sense of our sensory faculties being intercepted in their natural attachment to the things about them as lures of pleasure, and in their recoil from things as threats of pain. For the command that commands our thought to be in command commands our sensory faculties to expose themselves, not to the pleasurable or painful affects left on us by the things of the environment, but to their objective properties, the sensuous patterns inasmuch as they can be identified objectively and correlated rationally. This produces in our sensuous will, which is not anaesthetized but held in abeyance and reduced to passivity, a sense of frustration, of suffering. This suffering is the inner evidence we have of the inclination that thought, bent under the weight of the imperative, puts on our sensibility.

Thought is commanded to be in command, to command its own sensory-motor faculties. It must order one's sensory-motor faculties in such a way that they can collect data from the environment in comprehensible and regular ways, that they can measure the forces and obstacles and causalities of the practicable field in comprehensible and regular ways, and that they can register the relations of command and obedience that regulate the social order in comprehensible and regular ways. For one can sense one's diverse limbs and sensory surfaces reacting to whatever pressures affect them, adhering to whatever pleasurable contacts lure them. One has to then integrate one's sensory-motor powers in such a way that one can advance comprehensibly into nature, into the practicable field, into the social order.

To do so one has to *double up* the actual perception one can have of oneself at any moment with an advance representation of oneself, an image of the figure one will form while acting in nature, in the practicable field, and in society. These images Kant names "types." They are practical images; they are not representations of what one is but advance diagrams of the agent one must make of oneself.

The images one forms of one's sensory-motor powers integrated in action are formed by analogy with the totalities, regulated by law, one knows. These totalities are nature, the practicable field, and society. One has to form an image of oneself as a multiplicity of elements regulated, like a nature, with universal and necessary laws. One has to form an image of one's limbs and organs laid out, like a practicable field, as a system of means at the service of thought. And one has to form an image of one's faculties as a multiplicity of agencies ordered, like a microsociety, in relations of command and obedience.

These images are not produced by empirical observation of oneself. They are not produced by the investigation of the empirical laws that integrate one's organism and one's sentient nature, of the mechanical laws that regulate one's nervous circuitry and musculature, or of the sociobiological laws that govern one's nature as a gregarious animal. It is not through ever-greater understanding of the physico-chemical laws of universal nature that one will obtain an image of oneself as a nature able to explore nature. The advance of mechanical and technological understanding will not provide one with an image of oneself as a set of means able to manipulate the practicable field. The advance of ethnobiology will not one day make one see oneself as a microsociety of faculties able to produce a representation of the economic, juridic, and political order of society. The practical images of oneself that one forms when one acts are instead produced from within, diagrammed by thought in obedience to its own imperative. They are the images of oneself that one has to produce in order to envision acting in nature, in the practicable field, and in the social field in obedience to the imperative. They are images, produced immediately, that make it possible for thought to conceive of itself as being in command and thus being able to obey. They displace the image of oneself produced by empirical observation of one's nature, by practical observation of the utility of one's limbs and organs, and by social observation of one's moves in the social field.

They are practical images, imperative images. As one acts in one's sensory environment, one does not perceive one's organism as a sensitive mass reacting spasmodically to sensory substances promising pleasure or emitting pain, but imagines one's sensory surfaces oriented and focused by psychophysiological regulations proper to one's own nature. As one maneuvers in the practicable field extended about one, one does not perceive the masses of one's limbs reacting to the physical forces that they collide with, but imagines them operating as instruments at the service of one's own ends. As one advances in the field where others perceive and act, one does not perceive one's limbs reacting to physical forces only, but imagines them responding to commands; one imagines oneself obeying the orders of others because one's limbs and members obey the orders given by oneself.

The individual who sets out to make his disparate sensory and motor powers, reacting episodically to the lures of sensory apparitions that form and dissolve about him, into a nature, a totality regulated by laws; into a set of powers subordinated to his rational faculty as means to end; into a microsociety of powers regulated by relations of command and obedience— who sets out to do so in action, in practical life, through his purposive undertakings and through work—makes himself a work in something of the sense an artwork is a work. That is, a product that is finite, finished in itself, enclosed within boundaries which are its completion, self-containment, and perfection.

Exterior to us, we encounter the others. Our fellows pass by us. They take form among the sensory surfaces in our environment. They also face us, as others. They demand to be recognized as other than the sensory impressions phosphorescent in our own sensibil-

reality (?) governed by laws

ity. To recognize the other, Kant says, is to recognize the imperative for law that rules in the other. To recognize the other is to respect the other.

Here we can distinguish between what we can call a depth-perception of the other and a surface-sensitivity to the other. By a depth-perception of the other, I mean the per-ception that views the colored and palpable surfaces of the other as surfaces of a physiological and biological depth; sees these surfaces shifting, tensing, and relaxing and divines, beneath them, muscular contractions maintaining equilibrium; sees these surfaces breathing and sweating and divines, beneath them, glandular functionings, circulatory currents, a specific metabolism. Perception senses also tensions, drives, and compulsions that wrinkle this brow, tense these fists, focus these eyes. This perception extends on behind the substance enclosed with these surfaces, to the depth of the world behind it—envisions the road the other has traveled, the obstacles he has cleared, the heat of the sun he is fleeing. Perception perceives through the surface turned to us, into the depth of the organism and into the depth of the world.

This perception requires the thought that will elaborate biological and physiological concepts and laws so as to understand the secretions and movements observed on the other's surfaces, and will elaborate psychological concepts and laws so as to understand the drives and desires sensed in his grimaces and postures. This perception requires the psychophysiological concepts and laws that represent his drives and desires as connected with biological and physiological processes in his sentient and self-moving organism. It requires the thought that will elaborate physico-chemical concepts and laws to understand the material world behind him, the road he is walking, and the forces that open before, support, or obstruct his movements. It requires the microbiology and organic chemistry whose concepts and laws will make this organism intelligible as a part of material nature.

The posture and movements of the other, as one perceives them, do not only show position and displacement coded by physical and physiological laws; they also show a cultural coding. The other stands in military erectness, moves with Japanese glides, nods with Turkish affirmation and negation, shrugs her shoulders and purses her lips in French kinesics, sits on chairs in Victorian demureness or on his haunches in Indian posture. The other smiles in the bureaucratic or secretarial manner, laughs at accidents the Javanese way, feels Christmas joy or Songran hilarity, or feels Islamic indignation and Scandinavian loneliness. When the other speaks, it is with the tongue of a nation, the intonation of a class, the rhetoric of a social position, the idiom of a subculture, the vocabulary of an age group. When one perceives the other, one sees behind her posture and movements the demands of a job, the codes of etiquette, the history of a na-

tion. One sees behind his feelings the structure of hi-
erarchies, the rites of passage of a culture, the polari-
ties of ideologies. One envisions behind her speech
the semantic, syntactic, grammatical, and phonetic
patterns of a cultural arena and a history. The depth-
perception of the other requires the thought that represents the concepts and laws of disciplining, educa-
tion, job training, professional etiquette, kinesics, lin-
guistics, and ultimately ethnobiology and animal
psychology.

The forms of this thought are required by the approach of the other, as a surface that forms over a
material substance, taking form in a field of structures
and forces. Understanding represents the forms and
movements of the others as subject to psychological,
physiological, and physical laws and linguistic,
kinesic, and cultural codings. To understand the other
is to understand these laws and these codes as imperative for one's own understanding.

But the other is also *other*. To recognize the other
as other is to sense the imperative weighing on his or
her thought. It is to sense its imperative force—a force
that binds me also.

To recognize *the other* is to see his or her position
and movements as commanded by a representation
his or her thought formulates for itself in *subjection
to its own imperative*. It is to see his position, not as
produced by the laws of gravity and his movement,

not as effects of physical pressures, but as produced
by a representation his thought formulates for his will.
It is to see her posture ordered, not by the codes of
her culture, but by what she sees as her task. It is to
see his clenched fist or expansive smile, not produced
by biological drives or psychological compulsions, but
by representations of the desirable and the imperative
his thought formulated. It is to see her formulations
and expressions, not as instances of professional
training or ethnic codings, but as issuing from her
own representation of what is required and what is
proper.

I do not see the causality his representation would
have on his nervous circuitry and musculature; I indeed do not see the representation the other forms
in his mind. The command weighing on him, that he
formulate a representation of what is required and
command his sensory-motor faculties with that representation, is also not a hypothesis my thought finds
itself required to formulate in order to make his posture, moves, and words intelligible to me. For my perception of her organic processes and of the physical
and cultural field behind them has to be understood
in terms of psychological, physiological, and physico-
chemical laws. I am obligated, by the imperative
weighing on my thought, to explain each of her positions and moves by the universal laws regulating or-
ganisms and physical bodies, to explain each of her
gestures and words by the laws of psycholinguistics

and the codings of culture. I am obligated by the imperative weighing on my own thought to see him or her as real, that is, as an integral part of reality and regulated by the universal laws that make the spectacle of surface appearances about me nature. I have to assume that any irregular and unpredicted moves they make or words they utter are explainable by empirical laws, just as, Kant says, I am obliged to hold that an apparently irregular movement of a planet is explainable by the laws of astronomy.

What initiates that other vision of him or her, that sense of his or her surfaces as commanded by another law—that represented by his or her own mind in obedience to its own imperative—is the immediate sense I have of the imperative in him or her. To sense what weighs on his or her thought as an imperative, and not as a natural causality, is to sense it as a force imperative for me also. I find myself afflicted with the imperative that commands the other. I feel its weight as a force that weighs on my own understanding. I find myself compelled to see his or her surfaces as ordered surfaces, exposed to me and ordering me, that is, facing me.

This sense of an imperative in him or her that weighs on me also is immediate; it is not a hypothesis introduced at some point of an understanding of his or her position and moves as produced by intraorganic and intrapsychic depths and the depths of nature and culture behind him or her. The sense of an imperative in the other interrupts that understanding from the first. The sense of his or her surfaces as the surfacing of an order facing me displaces the perception of his or her surfaces as the surfaces of an organic and natural depth.

This is why it can happen that with the least glimpse at the other—the momentary glimpse at the slum child in the street as my car drives by, the momentary dull glint of the beggar's eyes in the dark as I head for the restaurant—I can feel arrested in my own intentions, contested. When I then elaborate a representation of what faced me, situating the surface I saw in the depth of biological and psychic drives beneath it— the animal avidity, the reflexes conditioned by passing strangers—and by situating it in the depth of culture behind it—the conditioned codes of the indigenous before the passage of foreign tourists, the immigrant's faulty command of the laws of etiquette and of the laws of grammar in my language explaining the raw force of the words he used, the sense of another imperative dissipates. My sociological, political, anthropological, and biological understanding reestablishes my imperative alone on my thought; my explanations justify my own understanding and my own intentions.

The imperative I sense commanding the position of the other weighs on me as immediately as the imperative my thought finds on itself; I sense it in the same sense of respect with which my mind senses the imperative for law weighing on itself. But it is *another*

imperative, contesting the imperative my thought has
always obeyed.

   What is it that locates for me the alien imperative
on the surface of the other which I see in the midst of
the order of nature, of the practicable field, and of
society? It is the sense of this surface as a surface of
suffering. In the measure that I sense the positions
and moves of the other, not resulting from the confluence of physical forces about him, not as simply
adjustments to the forces and shifts in his or her physical environment, but pushing against the hard edges
of reality, buffeted and wounded by them, I sense in
him an imperative other than that in obedience to
which I formulate the laws of nature. It is in the measure that I sense the maneuvers of the other, not as
simply movements of an instrument activating and ac-
tivated by the instrumental complex about him, but
striving to reorient the directions of force in the practicable field and wearied and exhausted by the forces
of things that resist him, that I sense in him an imperative for an order other than that of the finalities of the
layout of things. Inasmuch as I sense the gestures and
appeals of the other, not simply formulating the forms
required by the profession, the social status, the age
group, the etiquette, the circulation of information
and messages, but faltering, hesitating, and offended
by what is said, I sense in him an imperative other
than that with which I understand the laws and codes

of the social field. In facing me in the light of day, he shows wrinkles and wounds, in advancing in the practicable field, she reveals fatigue and exhaustion, in moving in the theater of society, he or she exposes his or her vulnerability to offenses and humiliation.

One does not, properly speaking, perceive this suffering. Sight positions the color and situates it at a distance; sight circumscribes the contours enclosing an exterior substance. Perception, that seeing-through which penetrates to apprehend the depth, does not see the suffering. The alien suffering does not extend at a viewing distance, but afflicts my sensibility immediately. It is felt in my eyes whose direction is confounded, whose focus softens, whose glance turns down in respect. It is felt in my hand that extends to clasp the hand of another as a manipulatable limb, but whose grip loosens under the sense of a sensitivity that touches me. It is felt in my voice that is in command of its own order and speaks to command, but which falters, hesitates, and loses its coherence before the nonresponse and the silence of the other.

The surfaces of the other, as surfaces of susceptibility and suffering, are felt in the caressing movement that troubles my exploring, manipulating, and expressive hand. For the hand that caresses is not investigating, does not gather information, is not a sense organ. It extends over a surface where the informative forms soften and sink away as it advances, where agitations of alien pleasure and pain surface to meet it and move it. The hand that caresses does not apprehend or manipulate; it is not an instrument. It extends over a surface which blocks the way to the substance while giving way everywhere; it extends over limbs which have abandoned their utility and their intentions. The hand that caresses does not communicate a message. It advances repetitively, aimlessly, and indefatigably, not knowing what it wants to say, where it is going, or why it has come here. In its aimlessness it is passive, in its agitation it no longer moves itself; it is moved by the passivity, the suffering, the torments of pleasure and pain, of the other.

What recognizes the suffering of the other is a sensitivity in my hands, in my voice, and in my eyes, which finds itself no longer moved by my own imperative but by the movements of abandon and vulnerability of the other. This sensitivity extends not to order the course and heal the substance of the other, but to feel the feeling of the other. The movement of this sensitivity recognizes the surfaces of the other as a face appealing to me and putting demands on me. It recognizes the imperative that commands the other ordering me also. What recognizes the suffering of the other is a movement in one's hand that turns one's dexterity into tact and tenderness; a movement in one's eyes that makes it lose sight of its objectives and turn down in a recoil of respect; and a movement *let your minds troubles give way to peace.*

in one's voice that interrupts its coherence and its force, confuses its concepts and its reasons, and troubles it with murmurs and silence.

The surfaces of the other, surfaces of suffering, that face me appeal to me and make demands on me. In them, an alien imperative weighs on me. The weight of the imperative is felt in the surfaces with which the other faces me with his or her weariness and vulnerability and which afflict me and confound my intentions.

Is there a difference anymore?

It is felt inasmuch as the surfaces with which the other faces me appeal to me as surfaces of exposure and vulnerability which call upon my resources. The other faces me with a turn of his or her eyes, exposing to me the nakedness of his or her eyes, unshielded and unclothed. Things—bare rooms, naked walls—derive their nakedness from the body that inhabits them; the nakedness of the body that denudes itself derives from the nakedness of the face. Only one who faces can denude his or her body; the one who turns to his or her tasks clothes his or her body with the skills of the deep-sea diver, the forces of the long-distance runner, the melodic veils of the ballet. In turning to me with the nakedness of his or her eyes, the other bares his or her face.

Some people mask their emptiness and their vulnerableness sorrow with a certain expressions. But some have a look and that triggers your response.

The other faces me with a gesture of his or her hand. The moves of his or her hand which address

◊ Now it depends not only on how you perceive them, but also on how they show you themselves, isn't it, allows you maybe?

me grasp on to nothing, form nothing, extend to me empty-handed.

The other faces me with his or her words. These words, which dissipate without leaving a trace, which are not an arm or an instrument, and whose force I can resist by doing nothing—by just doing whatever it was I was doing—are his or her way of coming disarmed and disarming.

With a look of her eyes, a gesture of her hand, and with a word of greeting, the other faces me and appeals to me—appeals to my welcome, to my resources, and to my response and responsibility. With the vulnerability of his eyes, with empty hands, with words exposing him to judgment and to humiliations, the other exposes himself to me as a surface of suffering that afflicts me and appeals to me imperatively.

The other can appeal to me because he can order me; he can call upon me because he can make demands on me. To respond to the other, even to answer her greeting, is already to recognize her rights over me. Each time I meet his glance or answer her words, I recognize that the imperative that orders his or her approach commands me also. I cannot return her glance, extend my hand, or respond to his words without exposing myself to his or her judgment and contestation.

The other comes as an intruder, and an authority, into the order of nature that my thought has represented in obedience to its own imperative; into the practicable field my thought has represented in a layout of means toward ends; and into the social field whose economic, political, and linguistic laws and codes of status and etiquette my thought has represented in obedience to its own imperative. He or she approaches as the surface of another imperative. His approach contests my environment, my practicable layout, and my social arena. Her approach commands an understanding that arises out of the sensitivity that is afflicted by her suffering.

When you arrived at the border, the guard at the gate said the officials had stopped working, for the lunch-hour. You pulled your car out of the sun and walked over to where there were some palmleaf-roofed shanties beside the road under the trees, to get something to eat yourself. There were eggs, tortillas, and refried beans. You sat down on a bench while the woman cooked them. A young man in camouflage fatigues asked if he could see your newspaper, which you had bought on the other side, in San José. The woman brought your lunch. You ate, opened your road map, and calculated the distances. You asked the woman for coffee. No one else was waiting to cross the border. The road dissolved in the boiling sun, and here in the shade flies buzzed lazily over rotting debris, skeletal dogs lying flat in the weeds panted. You looked at the soldier reading your newspaper. His lips were forming the words as he read, like a third-grade child. You could detect on his impassive face no reaction to what he read, no judgment on the interpretations of events he knew from his comrades who sleep uneasy nights in the swamps and forests and came back wounded or dead. The skin of his face was not mobile, nervous, like that of journalists and editorialists, but weathered like hide by a childhood spent, no doubt, laboring to harvest coffee, cotton, or sugar on a finca, and by months or years spent on guard in the cold fog of the cloud forests or in the swampy lowlands of the Mosquito Coast. His face and his hands were rough and scarred from exposure to the hot sun and the cold night winds, to the brush, and to the bullets of snipers—bullets paid for in Washington or in Saudi Arabia and shipped in from Miami, and from Israel, Poland, and China. His clothes were the camouflage dungarees and shirt of guerrillas everywhere, damp with sweat and clogged with dust. His shoes were not military, but were his own, that is, the rough rawhide shoes of laborers, of the land, of anyone. He was sitting near you, and said nothing to you. Only by his impassive face, his bared arms, his clothing, and his shoes, was he exposed to you. He had seen your gringo car waiting alone under the tree—you were one of those whose wealth and imperial politics had, in the six years of the proxy war, disappeared with bullets and mines within these borders 40,027 of his people, including 2,038 women, 1,996 children, 52 doctors, 176 teachers. As it said in your newspaper he was reading.

The hour was over, the border officials returned, and you drove on. That night, in your hotel in Managua, you thought again of him, standing there guarding the border post that had already been several times attacked by the Contras. Back home, months later, you continued to read, to put in perspective and to interpret the numbers of dollars, bullets, bodies, and the principles formulated to organize the numbers, to calculate practical directives out of them, and to make those directives intelligible to the writers and persuasive to others. It was to put another kind of distance between yourself and him. Your mind tracked down, surveyed, and reconnoitered lines of perspective extending across regional groups in conflict separated by mountain barriers or swamps in Nicaragua, across the walls and police lines that separated the fortresses of the rich from the slums of those who labor to make them rich, and across the barricades that separated the feudal dictatorship of the Somozas and the Latino socialism of the Sandinistas; you retraced the maps that design the interests of transnational corporations and those that geopolitical strategists lay out on tables in chanceries; you drew out of the past the lines of perspective that shape ancient Indian memories and the archaic forces of virile pride in villages made of mud in Central America. Your mind takes up numbers and dates and places computed on the dif-

ferent axes of these ecological, sociological, economic, geopolitical, and cultural spaces; your mind
reproduces within itself the taxonomies and the gram-
mars, the principles and the conclusions; your mind
generates interpretations, according to its own ad hoc
codes, which invest the formulations with ordering
force, judge, sanction and culpabilize.

Standpoints, positions your mind had established
from the distances of those lines of perspective, formulated in response to a disturbance, not his mute
voice; not his rational faculty, like your own, behind
the lips shaping the words of your newspaper like a
third-grade reader reading a fairy tale from another
land; not his body diagramming no stand and attitude
before you; but his face marked only by the brush in
the swamps and the winds in the cloud forests, his
hands mishandled by the land such that they barely
have the dexterity to turn the pages of a newspaper,
his rawhide shoes one with his fields and mountains,
have afflicted on you.

faces, idols, fetishes ▮

Modern epistemology set out to rigorously distinguish the real appearance of a thing from its perspectival deformations; its appearances in positions set askew or upside-down; obscured or confused appearances due to the poor lighting, the intervening medium, or the distance—to segregate the real appearances from illusory ones. Then it set out to demarcate the appearance given and perceived in a here-and-now presence from the traces of its appearance, retained by memory, of a moment before and from the anticipations of its appearance in a moment later. It set out to isolate the here-and-now given from the relationships between past, present, and surrounding appearances elaborated by the synthesizing operation of the sensibility that identifies something selfsame in a series of appearances extending across a span of time. This epistemology seeks to separate, in the multitude of appearances a thing extends in time and space, what is due to the reality of the thing from what is due to the intervening medium and what is due to the mind. It set out to inventory the pure data and to identify in the retinal imprints what is due to the thing itself.

The contemporary theory of perception declares this project infeasible. It is by converging our posture and sensory surfaces on something that it is perceivable. A thing reduced to its simple location in a here-now instant of presence is not visible or audible; an external thing is real by presenting itself in a wave of time and a field of extension, sending echoes and heralds of itself back into the past and into the future, and by projecting its form into us as an organizing diagram for our sensory-motor forces. Things are not reduced to their reality by being reduced to factual givens; the "pure facts" of empirical observation are abstracts of intersecting scientific theories, logics, and effects of technological engineering.

But things do not only project their appearances across different perspectives, in different media, and on the surfaces of our sensibility; they also cast shadows and form screens and phosphorescent veils; their surfaces double up into facades. They generate phantasmal reflections of themselves, refract off hints and lures, and leave traces.

The surface space of the purely visual, the range of harmonies and dissonances, the labyrinth of voluptuous contours and seductive hollows, the ether of obsessive presences and phantasms—these refractions off things are not private constructions built out of fragments of the core things or disconnected mirages that ill-focused eyes send to drift over the hull of the practicable world, made of substantial and graspable things. The practicable carpentry of things is itself suspended in their tectonic fault lines. These refractions off things are not private constructions in a space, which, like the invisible and impalpable space in which the community of scientists elaborates a representation of the world given in perception—a space we do not believe in and cannot inhabit, a space contained within us—exists only by hearsay.

It is because things turn phosphorescent facades on the levels and horizons of sensuous spaces that they also engender a graspable shape. What there is cannot be defined as a core appearance extracted by epistemological method, which can exist without its perspectival appearances, their doubles, masks, and mirages. The essences of things are not core appearances: it belongs to the essence of sensible things that they appear only in profiles and that their characteristics caricaturize themselves. A thing *is* by engendering images of itself, reflections, shadows, and halos. These cannot be separated from the core appearance which would make them possible, for they make what one takes to be the core appearance visible. The surfaces of things are not more real than their facades; the reality that engenders the phantasm is engendered by it. The monocular images, phantasms, lures, forms made of shadows, omens, halos, and reflections make the things visible and are the vis-

ibility the things engender. The echoes and the murmurs that wander off things, the odors that emanate
from them, the voluptuous contours and hollows of
things and of the waves and rain that caress, the
mossy forests and nocturnal fragrances that fondle
one's surfaces and penetrate one's orifices, and the
night they cast about their luminous outcroppings belong to the reality of things and make the things visible and real.

The things are not only structures with closed contours that lend themselves to manipulation and whose
consistency constrains us. They lure and threaten us,
support and obstruct us, sustain and debilitate us, direct us and calm us. They enrapture us with their sensuous substances and also with their luminous surfaces and their phosphorescent facades, their halos,
their radiance and their resonances.

It is by presenting ourselves, exposed visibly and
palpably in the light, that we engender the monstrous
shadow that precedes us and soaks into the ground
under our feet. The professor who enters the classroom the first day has been preceded by the legend
or myth of himself which the students now see materi-
alizing before their eyes. They adjust practically to the
level of his voice and to the arena of his movements;
he knows they are looking at the personage and fits
his person into it as he enters the room. He will use
this professorial mask as a fetish, to intimidate them.

They seek to penetrate beneath this mask, and their look finds the colors and contours of a caricature. If we recognize our acquaintances in the drawings made by the caricaturist, it is because our seeing was already not anatomical but caricaturizing. The perception that looks under the mask finds another, monstrous mask; the students see the pedant under the pedagogue. The look rebounds between layers of doubles that the face engenders. When the professor inspects his face in a mirror, his eyes are caught between the professorial mask and the pedantic caricature. When in the classroom he slouches over his papers and stifles a yawn, he is not simply shrinking back into a bare anatomy moved by fatigue, he is agitating his masks disdainfully or ironically.

When a face enters a room where people are gathered, borne exposed like an idol over a uniformed and coded body, marked with black and scarlet paint and adorned with flowers and the plumes of dead birds, the glances that turn to it lower or move obliquely across it. It would be hard to justify normalizing the practical imperative, hard to argue that the face whose clearly and distinctly exposed colors and whose firmly grasped carpentry is most palpably evident is the essence in which unpracticable forms of that face are absorbed, like monocular images in the real thing. A face is a face by not being a rubbery substance to be grasped and palpated or a skull to be handled gingerly like a costly china bowl; it is a face by commanding the downcast eyes that touch it with respect; it is a face by presenting the coded mask of a social drama. Mouth and cheeks, by idolizing themselves, are not jaws and jowls—or rather, jaws and jowls are the caricature that the mouth and cheeks double into. Is not the idolatrous look that reveres and profanes the face the norm, of which the anatomical and practicable scrutiny is a deviant? The face is the place of exposure and vulnerability of the organism; one does not look at feathery crystals in the moist membrane of the eye with the focus of a jeweler's eye which guides the precision movement of his adjusting hands; one look softens before the eyes of another, one's mobilization is disarmed; vulnerability and exposure order tenderness.

The face of the other is the surface of an organism, a surface upon which the anatomical inspection can follow the muscle contractions, nervous spasms, and blood circulation in the depths of that organism. The face of another is an expressive surface, a surface upon which the signs designating objects and objectives beyond can be read. The face of another is an indicative surface, upon which are spread indices of the moods and states of mind, the curiosity, doubt, skepticism, boredom of the other. The face of another is a surface upon which one senses directions and directives that order me; when another faces one, an imperative surfaces. The face of another is a landscape

of contours which are inertly expressive: heavy, over-
hanging brow; aquiline or infantile nose; thick, carnal
lips; weaseled or stolid chin; which the other, fixing
his dark-eyed stare or fluttering her eyelashes wet
with tears, learns to maneuver for effects.

The face of another also doubles up into an idol and
a fetish. To raise his or her face before the world is
to move among the others and the things as an idol
spreading its light and warmth over them; to set his
or her face over and against the others is to materialize as a fetish.

Sovereign and solitary, the idol glows with its own
light and radiates strange light and warmth about itself. It does not signal and give messages; the idol
gives force, gives not for asking, and gives without requiring anything in return.

The fetish is a caricature, not of the essential reality,
but of the idol. With the force of its downcast and
opaque coldness, it spreads black light and fevers
about itself. A fetish is used to obtain something one
needs or wants; it is put forth in the service of one's
fears or one's cupidity. The idol is noble; the fetish
is servile.

The terms idol and fetish are more often applied to
things made of noble or base material, to which a
face, derived from the human visage, is given. The
face that advances as an idol, before which the eyes
lower, turns into a mask and a caricature; the idol
made of stone or gold metamorphoses into a face that

keeps watch. But if the appearance of the human face can be cast on a thing, doubling it up into an idol and a fetish, that is because the human face first doubles itself up into idol and fetish.

The face, locus of expression and of valuation, is also locus of self-valorization—idolization. And, in a caricature of idolization, it also fetishizes itself.

The modern epistemology we have invoked has to say that the face of the other presents itself as a perceived datum—simple patches of color. The value the perceiver sees in it is a predicate he assigns to it. The relationship between a being and its value, including the relationship between a perceived carpentry of a face and the idol and the fetish it doubles into, is taken to be a predicative relationship and is studied in the grammar of axiological predication. Modern epistemology does not take this value as inherent in the face one perceives; instead, the value is a way of ranking it with regard to other faces and other things. The perceiver would possess a system of value-terms— good-bad, useful-useless, threatening-reassuring, etc. —with which he compares and opposes all things— and the face of another.

But does not the face of itself double into idol and fetish? The production of value-terms does not simply indicate or inform an idolization, but intensifies it. The ascription of predicate terms to itself to distinguish or oppose itself to others does not simply indicate or inform, but intensifies a fetishization. The value-terms with which it illuminates with marvelous light and ardor or spreads tenebrous fevers over the things and faces about itself, are terms first formed in this idolization, and fetishization, with which a face forms.

Let us look to the genesis of the value-terms that express idealization or, we shall say, idolization and fetishization.

Epistemology observes, given in culture, diverse sets of value-terms. It quickly says "value-systems", because when one looks at individuals applying these terms to the things and people about them, it seems that evaluation is ranking, and that it establishes gradation. It seems that value-systems are dyadic systems; for every value-term there is its opposite: good-bad, just-unjust, virtuous-vicious, beautiful-ugly, and useful-useless. These terms seem to be constructed as specifications of the most extreme kind of opposition, that of positive and negative. This absolute opposition would be what makes them intrinsically systematic; the meaning of the one can seem to be the simple negation of the other. The axes of kinship—male-female and parent-child—are not oppositional; the coexistence of a multiplicity of needy humans in a limited field of resources is, no more than the coexistence of a multiplicity of fish or baboons, not

intrinsically oppositional. It seems to us that the value-
terms in use are intrinsically oppositional systems and
that they introduce oppositions into the goods and ac-
tivities they evaluate. Among the other gregarious animals, even wolves and rats and the beasts of prey,
their gregarious nature prevents competition for
goods, territory, or prestige from becoming murder-
ous. But in the human species, gregarious animals torture and wage war on their own kind in the name of
values; value-oppositions make one see one's com-
petitor as an opponent, to be annihilated.

torture

But then value-terms do not simply discriminate and
classify. Their specific operation is not that of in-
forming by delineating (positing a representation by
negating, defining it by opposing it to other representations). They are forces. Forces not reacting to
boundaries, but acting on forces. An affirmative valuation is a confirmation. When we say to someone,
"How beautiful you are!" this saying does not work
on the one to whom it is said as a simple recognition
of what he is already, a re-cognition of what he already knows; it summons forth and incites his forces.
She will smile a gratuitous, radiating smile and a blush
will color her face more beautifully; she will move and
will speak still more beautifully in the space made luminous by the rainbow-colored word arching over it.
When we say to someone, "How sicko you are!" he
will outdo himself to grimace still more sickly and
mutter some still more sick retort. There are people

who never, or rarely, say "How beautiful you are!"
not because they, unlike the rest of us, never see every waitress, every bus-driver, every student, every
passing stranger as attractive or unattractive; or because they take seriously Jesus' recommendation,
"Judge not and you shall not be judged"; but because
they are all too aware of what you do when you say
that. All too aware that when you say that to your wife
it's a ploy or a compensation thrown her way, that
when you say that to a man you identify yourself as a
closet pervert, that when you say that to a student you
are laying yourself open to a sexual-harassment suit.

Hume introduced a new way of ranking ideas; he
ranked sensory ideas and abstract ideas according to
strength and weakness. But he then subordinated his
new ranking to the old one by valuing the strong impressions from the senses as more veridical than the
faint abstract images that are their after-effects, just as
Descartes ranked ideas according to their clarity and
distinctness only to see in the clarity and distinctness
of ideas the index of their truth. For Nietzsche, axiological discourse is completely separated from apophantic discourse. The beautiful words beautify, the
noble words ennoble, the strong words strengthen,
the healthy words vitalize; the ugly words sully, the
servile words debase those who speak them but also
those to whom they are spoken, the weak words
emasculate and debilitate, and the sick words contam-
inate. They do not only illuminate forms in the mind

of the one who understands them; they, like laughter heard that quickens and tears that trouble one, energize or unnerve the body in which they resound. It is because we see that our flattering or slandering words color and stiffen the corporeal substance of the one to whom we address them, even while his or her mind rejects them, that we believe our blessings and curses alter the course of things, even though our professed mechanism has long since isolated nature in itself from the enchantment of our voice.

Axiological discourse is not one language subordinated to or alongside of apophantic discourse; it is the primal one. The value-terms are not only the most important words of language, they are the stars about which the other constellations of language turn. Language is not fundamentally a means of identification, but a means of consecration. An infant is drawn into language, not because of the importance of saying, "It's the jam I want, not the butter," which he does not need words for, but because of the forces in the words *Love* and *Pretty Baby* and *Good* and *Yes*. It is through valuative words that the others intensify the world for him: good to eat, bad to put in your mouth, good warm bath, bad fire, pretty kitty, vicious dog, dangerous street. The most noble words in language are the most archaic; Homer only mentions three colors in all his epics—this is not explained by his blindness, because none of the epic literature of India, China, the Middle East, or the Yucatán mention any more. But we have hardly added much to the gamut of adjectives and epithets Homer used to exalt heroes. With the malice that understands what had been set up as the highest form of life by what was taken as the lowest, Nietzsche understands the most noble form of language, the language of values, as an atavistic survival of insect cries. Of course the language of gregarious insects, ants and bees, is representational, is governed by correspondence with the layout of things, and is a kinesics of truth. But language begins with the evolution of organs for vocalization among insects not socialized into colonies, whose vocalizations consist entirely of a seductive chant. Their organs for vocalization: scaly feet, rubbed thoraxes, and vibrating wings, radiate out a periodic, endlessly repetitive, vibratory chant whose repetitive codings are not representing, producing representations and ideality, but reiterating and reaffirming the forces of beauty, health, and superabundant vitality. Their vocalization is a gratuitous discharge of excess energies and the solar chant of expenditure without return.

Valuations are gifts of force given to the forces of things. It is with forces, welling up in oneself, that life confronts and opposes, but thereby incites, other forces. The strong sensations, those with which the force of life confronts what comes to encounter it, are not passive affects of pleasure and pain left on life by the impact of things that pass. The strong sensations are those with which an active sensibility greets what comes with laughter and tears, blessing and cursing. The cursing and the tears are themselves forces. The laughter and the tears quicken and trouble the landscapes, the blessing and the curses ennoble and unhinge the course of the world. The laughter is independent of the tears and comes before the tears; the blessing comes before the cursing. In the hands made for blessing, there is more force than in hands that claw at things unrelentingly driven by need and want. The recoil with which life discovers its weakness, and can resentfully will to weaken and appropriate, comes second. Life's blessing extends over a universe made of fragments, riddles, and dreadful accidents; it extends over them, not a nova of light in which they could be comprehended as one whole, their riddles solved, their contingencies revealed as instantiations of universal and necessary law—but extends over the dawn and the mists a rainbow of blessing that a fragmentary universe flourish and divide yet more, a universe of riddles extend its enigmas yet further, an accidental universe turn eternally in impermanence and transience.

Those who give the forces of value are those who have them, who have first given them to themselves. The value-terms, these new forces, originate in those healthy with a superabundant health: the passionate, the sovereign, the eagles, the Aztecs. The primary, positive and active, value-terms do not acquire their meaning in the grammar of indicative or informative speech acts, but in speech acts of the exclamatory form. They do not function to identify, to hold as identical, but to intensify. One arises from sleep, charged with energies to squander, one greets the dawn dancing over the trees, one greets the visions and mirages of the dawn, and the aborigine in one exclaims: How good it is to be alive! The goodness one bespeaks is a goodness one feels, within, in the feeling of excess energy, energy to waste, that is affecting itself and intensifying itself with each dance step one makes in the pas de deux that the dawn is choreographing. One says it because one feels it. And in saying it, one is not simply reporting on it; one feels good and feels still better for the saying of it. The goodness surges within and transfigures one's surfaces of exposure. One steps into one's bathroom; one's glance plays in the infinite echoes of one's naked body shimmering in all the mirrors like a quetzal bird, and one murmurs, How beautiful I am! One could only understand what "How beautiful I am!" means in the artist feeling for one's sinews and contours and carnality; in the selective, framing, and glorifying artist eye that captures and holds, as worth contemplating for years, an ephemeral event of nature: the shimmering and gratuitous grace of the morning mirage of oneself in the mirrors. And in saying that, one feels still more beautiful. One sees the beauty one's murmur makes reverberant in the shimmering image of one's punk mug, one's dirt-farmer skin. After the morning workout pumping iron in the gym to muscle exhaustion, one bounds up the steps to the street outside babbling, How healthy I am! One could only understand what "How healthy I am!" means in the force that would produce that exclamation in oneself. This health is not a negative concept, defined by the negation of its negative, like the capitalist who learns from the doctor's report that so far no ulcer, no degenerative heart disease, no cholesterol-clogged arteries; therefore you are healthy. This health is the feeling of force to squander gratuitously on barbells, on shadow boxing, and on racing the deer through the forests and the zebras across the savannah.

These exclamatory speech acts, in which the value-terms arise, are discontinuous vortices of force that redouble the spiraling vitality in which they arise. They are not arbitrary decrees of a legislative subjectivity imposing its own order and ranking on amorphous and neutral and indifferent material. The pot-bellied business-suited academic can lift up a glass in the end-of-term departmental luncheon and ejaculate, "I, one of the few, functionary of the celestial bureaucracy, how *kalos k' agathos* I am!": it doesn't take; his voice rings hollow in the muffled coils of his sluggish intestines stuffed with clots of cheese and cheap departmental wine.

The positive value-terms do not acquire the definiteness of their meaning from their definitions in a dyadic system. The goodness there, the superabundance, the gratuity, the excess over and beyond being there, is not a distinctive category that gets its meaning from its opposition to the reverse category.

The primary positive value-terms are not comparative; they do not function to differentiate an observed datum from its opposite, nor do they function to report on a comparative degree of change from a prior state one is recalling. When one exclaims, How beautiful I am! one is not noticing the differences between what the mirrors shimmer and what a mental photograph of the acned adolescent one once was shows; one does not mean that while the angle of my virile jaw is not up to that of the Marlboro Man, my gut is not as flabby as 53% of the other real estate agents and academics. When one exclaims, How healthy I am!, the meaning one knows in it is not determined by comparative observation of the exhausted and the stunted one contemplates in the rat-race of the wage-slaves glancing at their watches with anxiety-filled eyes in the street below; and one is not simply recording that, unlike yesterday, there were no shooting pains in the rhomboids even after ten reps on the cable row. When one exclaims, How good it is to be alive! one is not comparing one's big solid body with some miserable image of a clot of gray jelly one was before the cheap condom burst that night on the old man. The value-terms are not discriminations of differ-

What?

ence within a field maintained by memory. They are not effects that depend on the power of memory but productions that produce the power of forgetting. The woman from Puerto Rican Harlem who steps out from the gym and pushes her hard thighs down Fifth Avenue between the limp Long Island debutantes is not remembering childhood dysenteries and ringworms and dinners of boiled spaghetti; she knows she always was healthy, was conceived in health by her whore mother opening her loins one night to some dock-worker. The Lao youth who catches sight of his dirt-skinned punk mug blazing like a comet in the mirrored walls of the Bangkok disco and maliciously parades before the ravenous and fevered eyes of the rich white tourists like a prince before slaves is not remembering the stunted boy nobody deigned to notice in the muck of the plantation; he knows now he always was as splendid as the panthers that descended by night to prowl the plantation manor.

The positive and active value-terms do not acquire their use within language-games which are ways of socialized life, communication systems. Presenting themselves in an incantation, idols are mute to the others. These terms are not fixed in a system of opposition to their negations. For those of noble sensibility do not really have a sense of the bad, they do not really understand the morbid, the cringing, the rancorous, and the cynical. They look upon them with a look of pity that does not penetrate too deeply and that already feels contaminated by that pity. Bad for them means ill-favored, unfortunate. Their terms are not war-cries and slogans in a combat against the others; their vitality, health, beauty, and joy is not threatened by the multitudes of the impotent, and they have not made themselves feel joyous by inventorying the whines and complaints of others. They avoid them, and are unjust to them, out of ignorance.

There is not one dyadic system, where the positive value-terms are defined and posited by their negations; the denigrating terms are reactive, come second, and consecrate not excessive but morbid forces of life.

The servile are those who understand evil, and their morality is built around the notion of evil. Their central concept is this reactive and malignant concept. For by evil, they understand nothing else than the very image of those with sovereign instincts, who are felt to be dangerous by their own impotence, an image refracted and degraded in the acid of their rancor. The evil one for them is the one who is strong, that is, violent; beautiful, that is, vain; healthy, that is, lascivious; noble, that is, domineering.

This belligerent concept is not a simple opposite produced by negating the noble concept of good. The specter of evil is a strong and obsessive image, not simply a vacuous negation; it is the powerful creation of powers of weakness that have recoiled from confrontation and accumulate in rancor. Their eyes are fixed on the others, on the sovereign ones, and they understand them more deeply than they know themselves; they are able to envision in advance the whole picture of the sumptuous and horrifying flower of what is germinating in them. Their visionary artistry sees the Jezebel in the 4-year-old who paints his lips with his mother's lipstick, the snickerings of the world-dissolving Cartesian evil genius in a bunch of unruly kids in the ghetto school, the rapist-cum-axe-murderer in the strong arms of the chicano trying to hitch a ride on the highway.

It is the idea of good that is for them a pale after-effect of their sense of evil. They do not know it in their own instincts and their own joys but on their faces whose fearful and rapacious grimaces echo the words of the noble. In their lips, health means closure from the contagions of the world, beauty means enclosure in the uniforms of serviceability in the herd, goodness means productivity, and happiness means contentment with the content appropriated. It is we who live the good life, they say. But this goodness is itself a belligerent term, not an affirmation of gratuitous sovereignty, but a demand put on others.

Their forces, disengaged from the substances of things, recoil upon themselves and turn a surface of closure to the world. On this surface set against the others, the image of sovereignty is reflected and consecrated with rancorous and rapacious force as a demand put on the others. They face others representing values, face others with their fetishes, their faces doubled into fetishes.

We have been using words like *notion, concept, idea* of good, of health, strength, vitality, evil, and contentment. But the value-terms do not really designate concepts, forms which contain content or matrices which diagram essences. They are not terms which get their use and their definition from a structure of terms in systematic opposition, with which individuals determine and communicate their conceptually apprehended identities in opposition to one another. The servile sense of evil is not produced by simply using the grammatical operator of negation on the content of the noble and ennobling concept of good; the specter it invokes arises to consecrate and hallow a rancorous recoil of life that feeds on itself and intensifies itself. It is not an instrument in a system of communication; it is a war-cry in an assault that advances by intelligence, that is, by cunning, deviousness, deceit, and entrapment. It does not communicate; it contaminates and spreads by complicity.

Every value-term is a consecration of an excess force by which a living organism disengages from its integration in the forces of its setting and from its subjection to the reproductive imperative that subordinates it to the genus. The health that is not simply determined and defined by the set of tests the doctor administers to detect the symptoms of disease and organic and psychic degeneration, the health that is invoked in an exultant feeling of power is an excess known in the squandering with which it is continually replenished. It is the health that does not characterize one's functional integrity, but is, essentially, many kinds of health, known and yet unknown: the health of satyrs and guerrillas. It is a pledge and not a report, it is the trajectory of a dancing star born of a churning chaos of excess forces. The life that values its beauty—the artist compulsion in its original form, which, according to Nietzsche, works with the noblest and rarest clay and oil, its own flesh and blood—jettisons its natural forms and the forms its artistry has made second nature, for the sake of unknown dreams and dances. Were it to fix its sense of beauty on forms now acquired or contracted, mummifying them, they would turn into the grimaces of a fetish. The life that values veracity opens each of its austerely-won convictions to every contestation to come. The life that values responsibility sees every response made as a settlement not responsible enough, that has to be subjected to still further demands.

The exclamatory speech acts that posit value-terms are intrinsically discontinuous and consecrate moments of expenditure at a loss. Values are terms in the name of which riches and capacities, assets and securities, edifices and institutions accumulated and conserved through months, years, centuries, are squandered. They arise not in compulsions to realistically adjust to reality, but in compulsions to discharge one's forces and resources, in the exultation of the solar consummation flaring up in the immensities of the cosmic voids.

Value-terms, then, are not designations of a fixed order of forms that transcend space and time. They do not introduce into the beginningless, endless, flux of empirical events a factor of abiding permanence and conservation. They are not idealizing ideas; they do not function to idealize oneself, to fix one's presence in an abiding, selfsame form—an ideal presence. That is why we use the term idolizing: an idol exists in apparitions which do not fix the order of a common discourse, but glows with its own light that radiates light about itself and gives force, gives not for asking, gives without requiring anything in return.

Value-terms are not understood in mental acts which operate the systems of information and which delineate the meaning of one term more and more decisively by delineating more exactly the meaning of the other terms; they spread by contagion and spread contagion. The war-cry with which the healthy, the powerful, the proud, and the joyous are designated as evil does not convey information; it infects the language and it is picked up like a virus. When President Ronald Reagan identified President Daniel Ortega Saavedra as a "two-bit dictator in designer glasses," he spread an old man's rancorous castrating hatred of a young revolutionary to millions, confirming them in their belligerent ignorance. When a divemaster ascending from the Java Sea reports to the waiting boat, "Narked!" the rapture of the deep spreads to them, already, as they don wet suits and buckle weight belts.

One describes, as descriptively as possible, even clinically, the scene in the Bangkok cabaret where the seventeen-year-old Lao waiter suddenly climbed on a table and dropped his livery uniform on the plates and the glasses, his body heaving with abandon, his gorged erection throbbing at eye-level of the white-haired sapphire wholesalers and silkclad fashion designers—then, as your listener awaits your appraisal, the word "Wonderful!" or "Wow!" breaks the narrative. This utterance does not classify the narrated event in a judgment according to the social and normative codes; it exclaims that what was just narrated—what had never before been done or seen—was outside all the codes and norms with which one judges what one sees. It communicates to your listener by its tone—communicates something more than, and something different from, what the description, photographic and clinical as you could make it, communicated. Something unavowable, unconfessable, infantile and perverse—your involuntary, searing envy; your miserable pity that abruptly welled up—pity for your own seventeenth year, of child abuse; your seventeenth year in which your erections were shameful, guilty, hidden in the odors of urine and shit

of locked toilets; your seventeenth year when your
coming into biological, sexual maturity was sealed
with castration. And in your listener, who listened to
your description as the description of something he
or she had never seen or heard of or imagined, whose
somewhat frightened, scandalized mind was teeming
with social, ethical, normative judgments and con-
demnations, suddenly blushed with the heat of the
contagion of that feeling your word infected him or
her with. Something was understood; something was
understood between accomplices. Something was
said that made the other your accomplice.

The surfaces of another, which can be scrutinized
as an expanse of symptoms of the inner musculature,
glands, and nervous circuitry of the functional organism, double into a face. The face of the other is the
original locus of expression. The sensory-motor forces
that turn its contours and shape its movements speak,
are intentional, designate objects and objectives of
the environment.

At the same time, the sensuous forces that open the
eyes and the posture and expose the surfaces to the
landscape and that well up in superabundant vitality
and make the eyes radiant, the ears attuned to distant
melodies, and the face ardent, speak. The face re-
fracts a double of itself, made of warmth and light,
which speaks, not messages addressed to order others, but vitalizing and ennobling, confirming and con-

secrating words intoned to itself—words uttered not for their representational form but for their condensing, intensifying force—mantras. The expressive face doubles into an idol.

The forces that double up the one who turns his face to the world into an idol are not the intentional—cognitive and communicative—forces; they are sensuous forces that animate the surfaces of the other. For the sensuality there is in our sensitivity is not simply the affective effects by which the impact of outside stimuli, which are recorded as information-bits, double up into irradiations of pleasure and pain on our sensory surfaces. Pleasures and pains designate only the reactive affects of a passive sensibility. Sensuality in our organism is force and active; with the intensities of our sensuality, we turn to expose our bodies gratuitously to things our organism does not need to compensate for its needs and its wants; we open our eyes to distant vistas and mirages and to the most remote stars, and we open our ears to the hum of the city and the messageless murmur of forest insects and rustling leaves; we fondle the silk of robes and the powder of the butterflies still gaudy in death, and we expose our carnal substance to the grandeur of the oceans and the celestial terror of electrical storms. The strong and active forces of healthy sensuality are not pained by the absurd, but drive into it with the forces of laughter; they are not defeated by the mindless cruelties of the universe, but drive toward them with the forces of weeping and curses. The strong and active forces of healthy sensuality speak, speak words of consecration and imprecation.

The strong and active forces of sensuality on the surfaces of the expressive face double it with the laughter and tears of an idol. And speak their exultant and ennobling, consecrating, words. These words uttered by nonteleological, repetitive, insistent, intensifying forces chant and do not discourse. They do not designate what anyone sees, but make visible an apparition over the one that utters them. Words of joy and of lamentation which do not compare this apparition with others or address it to the demands or resources of others, they are sovereign words—mantras with which an idol crystallizes and sends forth flashes of light.

In the weak, passive sensuality there are also forces, rancorous and belligerent forces, and not only passive affects of pleasure and pain. The bitter and reactive sensuality rubs over its wounds and scars until they shine; it represents itself with the image of the good life in order to badger the others—fetishizes itself. It seeks to fix the ebbing forces of life with fixed forms, abiding and selfsame. Its idealizing words are fetishizing messages—demands addressed to others. The one who understands them understands their forces—that is, they spread not by their forms being comprehended by the discriminating and identifying intelligence of others, but by their cunning finding accomplices in the severe sensuality of others.

It is on the faces of others that we discover their values. It is not in the meaning of their expressions but on the figure they materialize, shaped not by the pressures of the world but by the joyous or rancorous inner force in them, that we see what their sensuality idolizes or fetishizes.

When someone coded in the common codes of civilization turns up and faces us, his or her face says, "Here I am!" He or she faces not simply as another particular upon which the social categories are instantiated. What faces is what the meaning one might give to this surface cannot contain, an excess over and above the forms and their coded significance. The facing is an exclamatory act that interrupts the exchange of messages picked up from others and passed on to others.

The I, the idol, that makes an apparition, saying, "Here I am", is not understood in an act of understanding that delineates the meaning of the term *I* by delineating how the he, she, and they who are around are coded. One abruptly finds oneself confronted by the apparition of the solitary animal: the eagle, the falcon, the satyr, the sphinx, the separated, the sacred one, the idol. To recognize what makes its appearance is not to re-cognize, to recode another instance of a category; it is to respond to the singular apparition.

The "Wow, it's you!" with which one responds is an exclamation that breaks the commerce of messages and that responds with a surge of sensuality and with a greeting that is laughter or weeping, blessing or cursing. An exclamation that, by its tone, communicates.

Something passes between one sensuality accomplice to another. Something was understood; the *password among accomplices* was recognized. Something was said that made you the accomplice of the one that is one of his kind: quetzal bird, savage, aboriginal, guerrilla, nomad, Mongol, Aztec, sphinx.

the murmur of the world ■

*W*e communicate information with spoken utterances, by telephone, with tape recordings, in writing, and with printing. With these methods we communicate in the linguistic code. We also communicate information with body kinesics—with gestures, postures, facial expressions, ways of breathing, sighing, and touching one another. The communication here too uses abbreviations, signs, and conventions.

To make drawn lines into writing, we have to conform with the convention that dictates that certain strokes correspond to a certain word and notion. Even those among us with excellent manual dexterity, good training, good health, and alertness make slips in our penmanship and our typing. There are always typos in the many-times copyedited critical editions of classic authors. There is no speaking without stammerings, mispronunciations, regional accents, or dysphonias. Typing and printing are designed to eliminate the cacography, yet in every book we have seen some letters and words that are so faintly impressed that they are inferred rather than seen. Recording, and radio and television transmission, are designed to eliminate the cacophony, but there can be static, cut-offs, and jamming; there is always hysteresis, the lagging of transmission due to shifting in the electromagnetic field; and there is always background noise.

Entering into communication means extracting the message from its background noise and from the noise that is internal to the message. Communication is a struggle against interference and confusion. It is a struggle against the irrelevant and ambiguous signals which must be pushed back into the background and against the cacophony in the signals the interlocutors address to one another—the regional accents, mispronunciations, inaudible pronunciations, stammerings, coughs, ejaculations, words started and then canceled, and ungrammatical formulations—and the cacography in the graphics.

COMMUNICATION AND CONTENTION

It is striking that the development of knowledge is conceived in military terms, such as *hunt, raid, strategy, battle,* and *conquest.* Yet is not knowledge developed in and for communication? When individuals shielded and armed encounter one another and make a move to communicate—extending bared hands and speaking—their violence comes to a stop. Discourse interrupts violence and words silence the clash of arms. Communication finds and establishes something in common beneath all contention.

But communication itself has been classically conceived as an agon, a contention between interlocutors. Communication takes place in discourse, that is, a dialectics of demand and response, statement and contestation, in which interlocutors oppose one another.

One sees communication as a continuation of violence, but with other means. One sees in the dialectical cadence of communication, proceeding by affirmation and contestation, an interval in which each makes himself other than the other, when one sees each one speaking in order to establish the rightness of what he says. To speak in order to establish one's own rightness is to speak in order to silence the other. Yet Socrates from the beginning excluded the possibility of establishing one's own rightness. Communication is an effort to silence, not the other, the interlocutor, but the outsider: the barbarian, the prosopopoeia of noise.

Michel Serres argues[1] that there is indeed force being exercised to resist and silence another in all communication, but it is not in the dialectic of demand and response, statement and contestation, in which interlocutors position themselves and differ the one

1. Michel Serres, "Platonic Dialogue," trans. Marilyn Sides in *Hermes*, ed. Josué V. Harari & David F. Bell (Baltimore: The Johns Hopkins University Press, 1983).

from the other. What the one says may oppose—
question, deny, or contradict—what the other says,
but in formulating opposing statements that respond
to one another, interlocutors do not entrench themselves in reciprocal exclusion. For speaker and auditor
exchange their roles in dialogue with a certain
rhythm; the source becomes reception and the reception, the source; the other becomes but a variant of
the same.[2] Discussion is not strife; it turns confrontation into interchange.

However, when two individuals renounce violence
and set out to communicate, they enter into a relation
of non-communication and violence with outsiders.
There could well be, and in fact always is, an outsider
or outsiders who have an interest in preventing communication. Every conversation between individuals is
subversive—subversive of some established order,
some established set of values, or some vested interests. There is always an enemy, a big brother listening
in on all our conversations, and that is why we talk
quietly behind closed doors. There is nothing you or
I say to one another in conversation that we would
say if the television cameras were focused on us for
direct broadcast.

There are outsiders who have an interest in preventing *this* rather than *that* from being communicated; they do so by arguing for that, by presenting it

2. Ibid., p. 67.

in seductive and captivating ways, or by filling the time and the space with it. There are outsiders who have an interest in preventing us from communicating at all. They do so by filling the time and the space with irrelevant and conflicting messages, with noise.

Formerly the street walls of buildings were blind, without windows; anyone who came to speak had to ring a bell and tell his name. Today the street walls of buildings are screens upon which messages are writ- *advertisements = noise* ten in neon flashes—irrelevant and conflicting messages which are not received and responded to but which agitate and merge into images that dazzle, inveigle, and excite the consumer frenzy of contemporary life. The roads and the paths to the furthest retreats in the country are lined with wires tense with stock-exchange pandemonium; beams bounced off satellites in outer space penetrate all the walls.

The walls we have to erect about ourselves are immaterial walls, the walls of an idiolect whose terms and turns of phrase are not in the dictionary and the manuals of rhetoric. Not only the talk of lovers, but every conversation that is resumed again and again becomes, over time, incomprehensible to outsiders. There is secrecy in every conversation. In the measure that this wall of secrecy gets thinner, we more and more utter but current opinions, conventional formulas, and inconsequential judgments. Heidegger quite missed that; it is the big and little Hitlers lurking in every hallway, every classroom, and every bar where we went to relax and get our minds off things, that produce *das Gerede*—"talk."

There are also allies—outsiders who have an interest in promoting the communication between us. The company wants the section members to communicate with one another; in disputes the police want us to try to communicate with our neighbors before calling them. Even authoritarian governments want the citizens to communicate at least their fears and resignation to one another.

When we cannot communicate, we appeal to outsiders to help. We enroll in classes, to learn from professors mastery of the established forms of discourse and the state of the current debate, so as to be able to communicate our insights effectively. We appeal to the scientific community, its established vocabulary and rhetorical forms, in trying to communicate with fellow-scientists from Japan or agricultural workers in Africa. Descartes, having established the existence of his own mind and his own thoughts, then appeals to the great outsider, God, before he moves on to consider the existence of other minds and the possibility of communicating with them.

In making philosophy not the imparting of a doctrine but the clarification of terms, Socrates, like analytic philosophers, like recent pragmatic philosophers, makes philosophy a facilitator of communication. Socrates, who evolved from soldier to philosopher in the service of the community, struggled against the babble and the barbarian who is the real enemy of truth.

But Michel Serres interprets the Socratic effort in such a way as to make the elimination of noise, in the rational community, a struggle against the rumble of the world and to make the struggle against the outsider a struggle against the empiricist.

(handwritten margin notes: Babel — confusion — prattle — communication — noise)

THE SIGNIFIED, THE SIGNIFIER, THE REFERENT

To communicate is to take an emitted signal to mean the same to the speaker and to the auditor. And it is to take an emitted signal to mean the same as a signal emitted before. The meaning designated by conventional signifiers at different times and in different places is recognized to be the same; Husserl characterizes the meaning of expressions as ideal. Meanings exist, not intemporally and aspatially, but by the indefinite possibility of recurring and by the indefinite possibility of being designated by signifiers issued anywhere, anytime.

There is, in language, no first or last occurrence of a word. A word can have meaning only if it can be repeated. The words that have suffered obsolescence can still be referred to, by linguists and students of literature, and can be returned to the language; their demise is never definitive. The first time a word is constructed, if it is to be able to enter into the usages of language, it must appear as already latent in the structures and paradigms and rules of formulation of the language.

It is not only the signification but the signifier, too, that is ideal. What signals in a sound is not its particular sonorous quality as really heard, but the formed sound that is taken to be ideally the same as that of other sounds uttered before and yet to be uttered. To hear sounds as words, to hear signals in the noise, is to abstract from the soprano or bass, thinness or resonance, softness or loudness, or tempo of their particular realizations and to attend only to the distinctive feature that conventionally makes the sounds distinct phonemes in the phonetic system of a particular language. The word as a signifier is already an abstraction and the product of an idealization.

Recognizing what is written involves epigraphy, a skill in separating out the ill-written features of the letters and words. The geometry class abstracts from the fact that the drawing the teacher has put on the board is only approximately a right triangle or a circle. When she draws a circle with a compass, one ignores the fact that the pencil angle shifts as she draws and the line is thicker on one side than on another. The reader systematically neglects not only the erroneous lines but also the particularities with which the letters have to be materialized. He disregards the fact that they are written in blue or black ink, or set in a Courier 10 or Courier 12 typeface. Reading is a peculiar kind of seeing that vaporizes the substrate, the hue and grain of the paper or of the computer screen and sees the writing as will-o'-the-wisp patterns in a space disconnected from the material layout of things.

To communicate is to have practiced that dematerializing seeing that is seeing patterns as writing and that dematerializing hearing that is hearing streams of sounds as words and phrases. It is to push into the background, as noise, the particular timber, pitch, volume, and tonal length of the words being uttered and to push into the background, as white noise, the particular color, penmanship, and typeface, of the visible patterns. Communication—by words and also by conventionalized kinesic signals—depends on the common development of these skills in eliminating the inner noise in signals and in dematerializing vision and audition.

To communicate with another, one first has to have terms with which one communicates with the successive moments of one's experience. Already to have a term which, when one pronounces it now, one takes to be the same as when one pronounced it a moment ago, is to have dematerialized the sound pattern, dematerialized a vocalization into a signifier, a word. Memory works this dematerialization. When one conveys something in words to another, how does one know that the communication is successful? Because

not respond you dont know if they understood you

one hears the other speaking about that experience, responding to it, and relating it to other experiences, in terms one would have used. To recognize the words of another as the words one used or would use, one departicularizes those words of their empirical particularities: their pitch, timbre, rhythm, density, and volume—their resonance. One disengages the word from its background noise and from the inner noise of its utterance. The maximal elimination of noise would produce successful communication among interlocutors themselves maximally interchangeable.

The meanings we communicate—the ways we refer to objects and situations—are abstract entities: recurrent forms. The signifiers with which we communicate are abstract, universal: ideal. But the referents, too, are abstract and idealized entities.

If we speak to another of a mountain vista, it is because that mountain landscape spoke to us; if we speak of a red, not brown, door, it is because that door emitted signals in the vibrations that made contact with our eyes. If our words, signals addressed to one another, have referents, it is because things address signals to us—or at least broadcast signals at large.

The medium teems with signals continually being broadcast from all the configurations and all the surfaces of things. To see that color of red, to pick up the signals from that door or that vista, is to constitute an enormous quantity of irrelevant and conflicting signals as background noise.

But to refer to that color of red with a word that one has used to refer to red things before and that will be used by one's interlocutor who does not see it or who sees it from his own angle of vision, is to filter out a multiplicity of signals given out by this particular door in the sun and shadows of this late afternoon and received by one who happens to be standing just here. What we communicate with the word and concept "red" is what, in this red door, can recur in other things designated by this word. The reception of signals from referents in view of communicating them is not a palpation that discerns the grain and pulp and tension with which each thing fills out the spot it so stubbornly and so exclusively occupies. It is seeing the red of the door, and the gloom of the forest and the shapes of the leaves, as modular patterns stamped on the unpenetrated density of things. Only this kind of leveling and undiscerning perception, Serres argues, could be communicated. "The object perceived," he complains, "is indefinitely discernible: there would have to be a different word for every circle, for every symbol, for every tree, and for every pigeon; a different word for yesterday, today, and tomorrow; and a different word according to whether he who perceives it is you or I, according to whether one of the two of us is angry, is jaundiced, and so on *ad infinitum.*"[3] To communicate is to consign to noise the teeming flood of signals emitted by what is particular, perspectival, and distinctive in each thing.

To abstract from the noise of the world is to be a rationalist. The first effort at communication already begins the dematerialization that thought will pursue. The effort to render a form independent of its empirical realizations issues in the constitution of the universal, the scientific, the mathematical.

THE CITY MAXIMALLY PURGED OF NOISE

We face one another to emit signals that can be received, recognized, and reiterated, while about us extends the humming, buzzing, murmuring, crackling, and roaring world. Our interlocutor receives the information by not harkening to the pitch, volume, accent, and buzz of our sounds, and attending only to the recognizable, repeatable form, consigning the singular sonority of our voice and sentence to noise internal to the message. And he turns to the thing, situation, or event referred to by our message as a recurrent and abstract entity, not as the singular vibrant density sunk in the morass of the world and emitting its particular signals, static, and noise. The

3. Ibid., p. 70.

practice of abstraction from the empirical implanta-
tion of things is what brings about communication. To
eliminate the noise is to have successfully received
the message. To communicate it is to reissue the abstract form. The abstract is maintained and subsists in
the medium of communication.

The community that forms in communicating is an
alliance of interlocutors who are on the same side,
who are not each Other for each other but all variants
of the Same, tied together by the mutual interest of
forcing back the tide of noise pollution.

The Socratic effort to communicate with strangers
is, in reality, the effort not to rationally certify the ex-
isting Athenian republic but to found an ideal republic
of universal communication—a city maximally purged
of noise.[4] It is an effort to found a scientific and mathematical discourse and to silence the rumble of the
world. In constructing an objective representation of
nature out of abstract mathematical entities, one produces a community in quasi-perfect communication,
a transparent Rousseauian community where what is
formulated in the mind of each is what is also formulated in the minds of the others. That community
would be imminent today, as all information becomes
digitally coded and transmitted by satellite in the silences of outer space.

4. Ibid., p. 68.

But is it really true that universal, abstract, objective, scientific discourse is departicularized and is the discourse of anyone? It can't be just accidental that to do philosophy is to compose one's own philosophy, a philosophy that will decompose with one. "If philosophy is autobiographical, in a sense that science is not . . . ," I was saying, when a philosopher of science interrupted me to refuse the distinction. "It is fatuous to say that if Einstein did not invent the special theory of relativity, someone else would have," she objected. "Everybody now understands that the data he was working with and the theories he was trying to integrate could be formulated and integrated in any number of different, imaginable and so far unimaginable, ways. If Einstein had not slipped out in time from Nazi Germany, there is every reason to think we would never have the special theory of relativity." The term "electricity" has a different sense for a television repairman than for an electrical engineer working on urban power generators or on CAT-scan equipment, but also for a meteorologist, a solid-state physicist, or an astronomer. Its meaning is different in each laboratory; the different models and paradigms with which any scientist works spread a different array of paths about the movement of his terms. It is not only the new hypotheses posited and new experiments devised that generate new conceptions; when a scientist reads the work of another scientist, the terms may generate a different movement in the paths of the conceptual operations of the reader than they had in those of the writer.

Is not, then, the ideal of the kind of maximally unequivocal transmission of messages in the industry of a social space maximally purged of noise that Serres invokes, another idol of the marketplace—idol of the communication theory (devised for the service of our military-industrial complex)?

Serres's argument leads him to identify, as noise, the whole of the empirical as such. "To isolate an ideal form is to render it independent of the empirical domain and of noise. Noise is the empirical portion of the message just as the empirical domain is the noise of form."[5] "The 'third man' to exclude," Serres now concludes, "is the empiricist, along with his empirical domain. . . . [I]n order for dialogue to be possible, one must close one's eyes and cover one's ears to the song and the beauty of the sirens. In a single blow, we eliminate hearing and noise, vision and failed drawing; in a single blow, we conceive the form and we understand each other."[6]

Rationalists—mathematicians, scientists, and the miraculous Greeks—eliminate the signals emitted by the particularities of empirical particulars and transmit only the abstract idealities; empiricists pick up all the static being emitted by the particularities of empirical

5. Ibid., p. 70.
6. Ibid.

realities and use different words for every circle and every pigeon, for the circles and pigeons others see from their perspectival points of view, and for circles and pigeons perceived with jaundiced eyes or the feline eyes of carnivorous interlocutors. They are Evil Geniuses of interference butting into every effort at communicating an unequivocal information-bit from one to the other. "The more [empiricists] are right, the less we can hear them; they end up only making noise."[7]

Empiricists are the demons that rule the world. But one cannot progressively assimilate more and more of these ephemeral proper names for the signals of the world; one has to struggle against them. The only solution is to say, with Leibniz against Locke, that "empiricism would always be correct if mathematics did not exist."[8] The community that establishes communication has to take its existence as proof of its validity. The only solution is to "not *want* to listen to Protagoras and Callicles—because they are right." This, Serres writes, "is not an *ad hominem* argument; it is the only logical defense possible."[9] The community we must want must not want to hear the glossolalia of nonhuman things—the humming, buzzing, murmuring, crackling, and roaring of the world, must not want to hear the stammerings, quaverings, dronings

7. Ibid., p. 70, n. 11.
8. Ibid., p. 70, n. 12.
9. Ibid.

of one another's voices, and must want its hearing perfectly adjusted to hear the mathematics relayed by satellites in outer space.

What an extraordinary outcome of the ancient Socratic philosophy of dialogue completed now in a contemporary theory of communication! The struggle for the establishment of transparent intersubjectivity is a battle against the relayers of the signals of the world. Communication depends on, is the other side of, non-communication—a *wanting* to not communicate and an active battle to silence the empiricist demons. The only logical defense of rationality and logic is the active and combative will to not listen to Protagoras and Callicles—because they are right!

THE ENCOUNTER WITH THE OTHER

 Serres conceives of communication as an exchange of expressions that have the same informative value for the receiver as for the emitter, expressions whose value reduces to exchange-value. Expressions that would discern what differentiates one circle from another; one symbol, tree, or pigeon from another; one yesterday, today, or tomorrow from another; or your angry or jaundiced perception from mine, have no communicative value. Serres then conceives of interlocutors as emitters and receptors which interchange their functions. In the measure that what was received was what was emitted and that what was communicated was the abstract, departicularized message, each partner in conversation becomes the same for the other: the auditor becoming speaker of what he heard and the receptor source of what he received.

Serres argues that in a dialogue, the two interlocutors are "in no way opposed,"[10] but are variants of each other, are variants of the Same, because the questioner and the respondent exchange their reciprocal roles, with the source becoming reception and the reception source, "according to a given rhythm." But does not this rhythm oppose them? Is it not the time-gap between emission of the signal and its reception that opens up the space of hysteresis where the interferences and the misconstructions enter? In the ideal republic that Serres invokes—the city of communication maximally purged of noise—would not the emission and reception have to be simultaneous? The less time involved in the communication means the less thermodynamic energy involved and the less entropy. Two modems, transmitting and receiving information-bits simultaneously, would be the model.

But to affirm something is not simply to make oneself the momentary source of a formulation whose abstractness makes it equivalent of what any interlocutor does or can issue and receive; it is to present some-

10. Ibid., p. 67.

thing to someone for his judgment, his confirmation or contestation. To set oneself forth as a subject of discourse is to expose oneself to being contested and discredited. To make oneself a subject in discourse is to subject oneself to another. Already, to greet someone is to recognize his or her right over one.

hiw?

To question someone is not simply to make oneself a receptor for information which one will soon reissue; it is to appeal to another for what is not available to oneself. To address a query or even a greeting to another is to expose one's ignorance, one's lacks, and one's destitution and is to appeal for assistance to one non-symmetrical with oneself.

To address someone is not simply to address a source of information; it is to address one who will answer and answer for his or her answer. The time delay, between statement and response, is the time in which the other, while fully present there before one, withdraws into the fourth dimension—reaffirming his or her otherness, rising up behind whatever he presents of himself, and rising up ever beyond whatever I represent of her and present to her—to contest it or to confirm it.

To enter into conversation with another is to lay down one's arms and one's defenses; to throw open the gates of one's own positions; to expose oneself to the other, the outsider; and to lay oneself open to surprises, contestation, and inculpation. It is to risk what one found or produced in common. To enter into conversation is to struggle against the noise, the interference, and the vested interests, the big brothers and the little Hitlers always listening in—in order to expose oneself to the alien, the Balinese and the Aztec, the victims and the excluded, the Palestinians and the Quechuas and the Crow Indians, the dreamers, the mystics, the mad, the tortured, and the birds and the frogs. One enters into conversation in order to become an other for the other.

THE NOISE IN THE MESSAGE

We are necessary as efficient causes of new sentences, producers of new information formulated with old words. But in our particularities, our perspectival points of view, and our distinctive capacities to issue and to receive meanings, we are part of the noise. The time it takes to formulate those sentences is a time filled with the opacity of our own voices. How transparent communication might be if there were not resistance in the channels that conduct it: no lilting, bombastic, stammering voice pronouncing it!

Yet is there not also a communication in the hearing of the noise in one another's voices—the noise of one another's life that accompanies the harkening to the message? What kind of communication would that be?

The particular, the material, the empirical, Serres says, is indefinitely discernible. It is a succession of signals, each with its own name, in a static that cannot be recorded or reproduced. Yet surely every day we do succeed in communicating to one another, not only the abstract formula of an insight, but the unique spell of the encounter with an early-winter afternoon, the charm of something someone said that was never before said, or the weirdness of a feeling never before felt. Language is the amazing power to say, with a limited number of words and grammatical structures, sentences never before said that formulate events that have never before occurred.

Every new sentence that succeeds in saying something does so, Merleau-Ponty said, by a coherent deformation of the sentence paradigms already in the language. Every new sentence also continues the bending, extending, and deforming of the code. "Let us agree," Serres writes, "that . . . communication is only possible between two persons used to the same . . . forms, trained to code and decode a meaning by using the same key."[11] But when an American, brought up on Indian legends, says to an Englishman, brought up on legends of imperial conquerors, "He's brave . . . ," they do not have the same key to this word. If, nonetheless, the one understands the other, it is by improvising the key as one goes along.

11. Ibid., p. 65.

Is it not also false to suppose that only the meaning attached to words by a code, fixed or evolving, communicates? The rhythm, the tone, the periodicity, the stammerings, and the silences communicate. In the rush of the breathless voice, the tumult of events is conveyed; in the heavy silence that weighs on the voice, the oppressive tedium of a place is communicated. " 'Prove it,' demands the logocentric system that the art historian worships. 'Prove that you still love me. . . . ' " Joanna Frueh, performance art critic, is saying it in different intonations, volumes, and crescendos—sparring with the voice of the academic demand, and circling around the male: "Prove it. . . . *Prove* that you still love me. . . . " "Prove that you still *love* me. . . . "

The noise of our throats that fills the time it takes to convey the message communicates the noise of the things or makes the things discernible in their empirical plurality. By the utterance of every insight we have into an empirical particular—a particular circle, tree, or pigeon we contemplated yesterday when we were angry or jaundiced—breaking into the universal circulation of passwords, watchwords, and orders; by singling out a particular interlocutor; and by interrupting the narrative or the explanation with an intonation, an attack and cadence, or with the redundancies that blur and interjections that wail, bray, or strike speechless; we do succeed in communicating the differentiation, the plurality of facets and of perspectives and the indefinite discernibility of empirical particulars. Anyone who thinks we are only emitting noise is one who does not *want* to listen.

The one who understands is not extracting the abstract form out of the tone, the rhythm, and the cadences—the noise internal to the utterance, the cacophony internal to the emission of the message. He or she is also listening to that internal noise—the rasping or smoldering breath, the hyperventilating or somnolent lungs, the rumblings and internal echoes—in which the message is particularized and materialized and in which the empirical reality of something indefinitely discernible, encountered in the path of one's own life, is referred to and communicated.

With this internal noise it is the other, in his or her materiality, that stands forth and stands apart making appeals and demands. The other is not simply the recurrent function of appealing to and contesting me; he or she is an empirically discernible vulnerability and intrusion. In *Visage* Luciano Berio composed not with words but with the sonorous elements with which words are formed—the sighs, gasps, waverings, dronings, hissings, sobs, giggles, whimperings, snivelings, screams, snortings, purrings, mutterings, and moanings—out of which, sometimes, words are shaped. He plunged them into a vast space in which electronic sounds hum, pound, sing, scatter, dissipate and where, finally, the roar of machines drowns out the human voice. In them, Cathy Berberian exposes herself more than her intentions and judgments could have revealed—exposes her sensibility, her susceptibility, her mortality, and the flux and scope of her carnal existence.

As efficient causes of expressions that convey information, we are interchangeable. Our singularity and our indefinite discernibility is found in, and is heard in, our outcries and our murmurs, our laughter and our tears: the noise of life.

THE BACKGROUND NOISE

If the neosocratic communication theory of Michel Serres has not understood—has not *wanted* to understand—the noise internal to communication: the pulse and the wobble, the opacity of the timber and density of the voice, the noise of life, the noise each of us is in his or her particularity; it has also not understood—has not *wanted* to understand—the background noise in the midst of which we speak.

Advances in soundproofing technologies and digital recording promise the complete elimination of background noise. Sensory-deprivation tanks were first invented in the '60s by John C. Lilly who was working with dolphins and, like every diver, loved the silence and the bliss of deep-sea diving and thought to dupli-

cate it on land. But the technology that eliminates the
noise also eliminates the communication. In the absence of auditory, visual, and tactual background signals, one no longer senses the boundaries between
outside and inside, past and present, perception and
images, and one soon hallucinates. If the reception of
a determinate signal is impossible beyond a certain
level of background noise, the intention to emit a determinate signal becomes unrealizable without a certain level of ambient drone to escalate, punctuate,
and redirect. Recorded white noise—forest murmurs,
the rumble of the city—was added to space capsules;
the recordings are sold to terrestrials living in sound-
proofed apartments.

We understand that background noise is essential
to communication when we understand that reception
in the communication system of our bodies is not the
passive exposing of a preprogrammed surface of sensibility to outside stimuli, but picking a signal out of
the multiplicity of irrelevant and conflicting signals.
Where the receptor organ can receive a wide variety
of signals, perception is the active power to focus in
on, isolate, segregate, shape a figure, and reduce the
rest to indifferentiation. If, each time we look, we see
a figure standing out against the adjacent objects, this
is not due to the physical stimulation that is being
spread across our retinas; it must be due to an active
power in our gaze. Since communication is, for the
receiver, actively separating a figure from the back-

ground, then in the absence of the background there can be no figure either. If one looks into a closed, elliptically shaped box painted black and uniformly illuminated with white light, one cannot see the black and cannot see the surfaces at all; all one sees is a luminous gray density. But if one then sticks a white strip of paper on the wall of that box, suddenly the light becomes transparent and the hue of the medium recedes and condenses into black on the walls of the box. When the psychologist seats a subject in a room such that he sees only the homogeneous surface of a broad wall uniformly illuminated, the subject cannot see how far it is from him, cannot see any surface at all, sees only a medium in depth about him, and cannot say what color it is. John Cage once emerged from a soundproof room to declare that there was no such state as silence. In that room he heard the rustling, throbbing, whooshing, buzzings, ringings, and squeakings with which the movements of his muscles and glands resounded with the ripples and rumbles of the never-ending movements of the atmosphere.

If the reception of a determinate signal is the segregation of a sonorous field into figure and background drone, the emission of a determinate signal forms in the hum of the field. Communication theory identifies the background hum as a multitude of irrelevant or conflicting signals. To designate it, thus, as noise is to conceive it from the point of view of the individual

teleologically destined to citizenship in an ideal republic maximally purged of the noise of life and of
the empirical domain—the miraculous Greece or the
totally transparent Rousseauist society. We shall conceive a different understanding of the background
noise if we put vocalization among us in the perspective of evolutionary biology.

One day, while trying to drive in the chaotic traffic
of Teheran, with each move I tried to make provoking
taps on the horns of cars beside, behind, and advancing toward me, I remarked to a hitch-hiker I had
picked up, that after five blocks of this I felt like a
road lizard on bad amphetamines. Oh, they are not,
like us Westerners, using the horn as a warning or a
threat, he said. They are like quail clucking as they
feed on a ripe wheat field. They are, he meant, creating a sound environment with which they symbioti-
cally merge with one another. I understood at once,
because my mind flashed back to the long nights I
had driven across Turkey and Iran when the next town
proved to take, not the hour I had calculated, but six
hours due to the devastated condition of the road and
the flooded rivers, and how I had thought that night
driving in a car is the absolute form of hermitage that
civilization had finally invented. When you are alone
in the middle of the night in a hotel room in an alien
country, you cannot moan out your loneliness and
misery without someone hearing you on the other
side of the wall, but if you are driving nights on the

highway you can scream and none of the cars crossing you in the opposite lane will hear anything. When I drive distances at night, I, like Simon Styletes on his pillar in the Egyptian deserts, invariably fall into extremist spiritual exercises revolving around the theme *Memento mori*, reviewing the meaning or meaningless of my life in the cosmic voids ahead. With the tappings of the horns, the yearnings or outcries of solitude penetrate the hull of roar with which one's car encases its motion, and merge and become common.

When one lives with birds one sees how the noise level of the birds keeps up with the noise level of the house, with the wind that begins to whisper and whistle across the sidings, with each notch up you turn the volume dial on your record player. It is the rumble and rasping of the inert things that provokes the vocalization of the animals; fish hum with the streams and birds chatter in the crackling of the windy forest. To live is to echo the vibrancy of things. To be, for material things, is to resonate. There is sound in things like there is warmth and cold in things, and things resonate like they irradiate their warmth or their cold. The quail and the albatross, the crows and the hummingbirds, the coyotes and the seals, the schooling fish and the great whales, the crocodiles infrasonically and the praying mantises ultrasonically continue and reverberate the creaking of the branches, the fluttering of the leaves, the bubbling of

the creeks, the hissing of the marsh gasses, the whir-
ring of the winds, the shifting of the rocks, the grinding of the earth's plates.

This noise is not analytically decomposable, as communication theory would have it, into a multiplicity
of signals, information-bits, that are irrelevant or that
conflict: that become, in Serres's word, *equivocal*.
The noise figures as resonance and vocalization that,
like the scraping wings of crickets we hear, contains
no message.[12] Olivier Messaien, in his *Chronochromie*, did not compose into music, into rhythm and
harmony and melody, the enormous quantity of signals being emitted by the birds of the jungle that he
had in his vast collection of tapes of bird cries; we
hear in *Chronochromie* the sounds of metals—cym-
bals, bells, blocks, pipes, and rasps; woods—mahoga-
nies, oaks, and bamboos; hides—cords and drums;
fibers—whisks; and strings, gums, and fluids trans-
forming into the wild exultant racket of multitudes of
feathered and flying things. And as we listen, it transforms again into our own sounds.

For we too communicate what we communicate
with the background noise, and we communicate the
background noise. The communication takes place
when the vibrancy of the land, the oceans, and the

12. Crickets communicate in the ultrasonic range, too high for
human ears to hear. Diane Ackerman, *A Natural History of the
Senses* (New York: Random House, 1990), p. 195.

skies is taken up, condensed, and unfurled in the hollows of one's body, then released, and when one hears its echo returning with the wind and the sea.

In the highlands of Irian Jaya it seemed that no matter how late it was at night, there was always someone who could not sleep and who spent his insomnia singing and drumming. "Are they preparing a ceremony or feast?" I asked a missionary with whom I had taken shelter and who was keeping me up for Christmas midnight mass. "No," he answered. "It goes on every night. In fact they are afraid of the night. They are like children," he said, with the weariness of his years. But their vocalizations did not sound to me to be issuing out of breasts where fear trembled. It seemed to me that their chants and yodelings picked up and reverberated sounds their own throats made, sounds other throats made, sounds the marshes and the birds of the night and the winds were making. J. M. G. Le Clézio lived long among the Indians in the Chiapas in Mexico and in Panama; to live among them is to live in the days and nights of their music: music made with bamboo tubes, perforated pipes, drums, shells, rattles, and also with a taut falsetto use of the voice, the throat having become a flute or whistle. Le Clézio heard it in the midst of the din of the rain forest: in the barking of dogs, the cries of the spider monkeys, the agoutis, the hawks, the jaguars, and in the vocalization of the frogs which fills the whole length of every night in the rain forest. It seemed to him that any

musicologist who just studied the tapes of Indian music in the laboratories, filled with synthesizers, in Paris
or Frankfurt would inevitably connect the specific
scales, pitches, rhythms, and phrasings of Indian music with cultural values and conventions and would try
to connect it with their myths and tragic cultural history. But theirs is a music made of cries and chants
without melody or harmony, a music not made for
dancing or pleasing; it is a music with which they see,
hear, and feel in the anesthesia of the night. "Melodi-
ous music is first the conviction that time is fluid, that
events recur, and that there is what we call 'meaning.' " But "for the Indian, music has no meaning. It
has no duration. It has no beginning, no end, no cli-
max."[13] Words are prisons in which the breath of life
is imprisoned in human form; in a music without melody and without meaning, the Indian hears the animal, vegetable, mineral, and demonic realms. One
had to listen to it there, in the nights of the Lacandone
rain forest, to understand that this "music" is not an
aesthetic production, that is, a creation of human subjectivities attempting to communicate immanent states
like moods, feelings, values, or messages to other human subjectivities. It is a prolongation of the forest
murmurs, the whispering sands, and the hum of the
heavenly bodies.

Separated   from   the   vocalizations,   rumblings,

13. J. M. G. Le Clézio, *Haï* (Geneva: Skira, 1971), pp. 51–52.

creakings, and whirrings of animate and inanimate nature, music becomes a means of communicating between humans only. Words can be added to it, speaking of the loneliness of individuals overcome through human love. But this communication in a city maximally purged of noise is a recent creation. A friend recently played for me, on his state-of-the-art equipment, a CD disk of the only complete recording of the Balinese Kechak. Listening to it, I was at once astonished and mesmerized by the purity, transparency, and beauty of the digitally recorded and cleansed sounds. But after a few moments, I began to think of how abstract it was; one was hearing only a tonal mapping of the Kechak, like reading the score of a concerto for harp without hearing the tinkling crescendos or seeing the elegant and aristocratic figure of the harpist seated there in the baroque concert hall of old Prague. I had never succeeded in doing anything but irritate anyone who was riding in my car while I had Balinese or Javanese music on the tape player, and I would apologetically explain that, in fact, I had myself come to be so captivated by this music because of the whole setting: drifting through the dark and wet jungle after the day's work is done; idling for an hour or two among the gossiping Balinese quite unconcerned that the players have not yet arrived two hours after they said they would; settling into the throbbing of the frogs and night insects; seating myself on the ground as the circle of seated men expanded and the priest lit the torches that awaken the monstrous figures of the demons that guard the temple compound while the incense stirs the spirits that slumber in the flowering trees and vines, and the glistening bare bodies of the men massed on the ground begin to sway as the trance, ancient as the sea, spreads among them, then abruptly their animal outcries greeting the apparition of the gods weaving among them: dancing gods, bound in exquisite silks and batiks, their heads crowned with delicate-stemmed flowers and smoldering sticks of incense and their jewels throwing off ruby and sapphire flash-fires. The digital recording, cleansed not only of the noise of the reproductive equipment but of the background noise of the performance, does not, I thought, reproduce perfectly the sounds of the Kechak dance; it creates music. Western civilization which created, in the eighteenth century, the market economy and, indeed, economic activity; which created the abstract universal essence of libido; which created people as female and as male; which created the value-free objective representation of nature and history and culture; which created sculpture out of African fetishes and created paintings out of tang'kas, those cosmic diagrams and instruments for centering in meditation found in Tibetan gompas; which created art, art for art's sake, out of ritual and civic ceremonies; has now created music out of the Balinese Kechak. The Balinese, for their part, have no word in their language for art and do not listen to the music; at night in the temple compound, they rock their squalling children, nurse them, chat with neighbors, go out to get something to eat, admire and severely criticize the performance of the fellow-villager who is dancing the Rama or the Sita, fall into trance, come out of it, are transubstantiated into gods, demons, rivers, storms, and night. In fact, when Bach composed, rehearsed, and directed a cantata, he was not simply creating music; he was praising God, earning merit and salvation, paying for the upkeep of his twelve children, competing with Telemann and Purcell, enhancing the status of his prince-patron and his own station, and contributing to a successful Christmas feast for all the town.

The creation, in our time, of music, like every cultural creation, is an inestimable contribution to the wealth of our heritage and makes, Nietzsche would say, this old earth a sweeter place to live on. The music was produced by the electronic elimination of all the marginal and subliminal signals coming from the nonmusical sonorous medium: the chatter of the village, the people, and the history; the remote murmurs and rumblings of the gods and demons; the barking dogs and the crowing roosters prematurely awakened from their somnolence by the dawn they see flickering from the torches; the night insects and the frogs; the rustling of leaves; the clatter of the rain; the restlessness of the air currents in the night skies; and the creaking of the rock strata—the background noise.

We too do not vocalize and mark surfaces only because we have some message to transmit. Significant speech, utterances where one can, like Serres, distinguish the calliphony from the cacophony, the message from the noise, is only an abstract part of speech. When grammarians and linguists analyze any text, they are astonished at how much redundancy there is in all speaking; how much of what we say to one another is repetition, chorus, murmur, and drawn-out resonance. We are no different from the celestial birds, who chime in with one another but know that it is only occasionally, in all this effervescent racket, that some information about a delectable kind of seed that got put in the dish today or some danger is being addressed to them.

You were dozing in your room and you woke, wondering what time it was. You thought, like that disheveled figure on a bed in the French cartoon that you had glued at eye view of your pillow, "Si je continue comme ça, je ne serai jamais maître du monde!" (If I keep on like this, I never will be the master of the world!). You tried to get the blood stirring and some movement started, you shuffled to the kitchen, shaking up some things on the way, making the door creak by opening it with a thrust, so as to get some movement in the dead silence of the house. You came upon your housemate sprawled torpidly on the couch, like a cold-blooded frog in midafternoon: "Hey, man, like, whatcha doing, huh?" Where is the information-bit? You said that to get some night sounds going, some rhythm going, some hopping about started.

It is out of and in the midst of the reverberation of ambient materiality that the utterances we make get shaped, and they get sent forth to return to it. The resonance of things animate and inanimate is in the redundancies, the drawn-out vowels and consonants, the hisses and groans and ejaculations, and the babble and mumbling and murmur that is the basso continuo of all our message-laden utterances.

Computer technology, driven by the pilot-industries of the military-industrial complex, places top priority on transmitting the message as effectively, efficiently, and effortlessly as possible. It is computer technology that shaped and forms contemporary communication theory.[14] But so little of what we say to one another makes any sense! So little of it makes any pretense to be taken seriously, so much of it is simple malarkey, in which we indulge ourselves with the same warm visceral pleasure that we indulge in belching and passing air. It really is, Nietzsche long ago pointed out, bad taste to make serious pronouncements and work out syllogistically valid arguments in civilized com-

14. The late works of Michel Serres are so many contributions toward a reinstated empiricism. See, among others, Les cinq sens (Paris: Grasset, 1985).

pany. So much of language added to industry and enterprises that are programmed by the laws of nature
or rational science and that operate all by themselves,
so much of language added to fumblings and break-
downs and even disasters has no other function than
to provoke laughter. Laughter mixing in moans,
howls, screams into the racket of the world. As much
of what we say when we embrace we say to release
our sighs and our sobs into the rains and the seas.

All these stammerings, exclamations, slurrings,
murmurs, rumblings, cooings, and laughter, all this
noise we make when we are together makes it possible to view us as struggling, together, to jam the unequivocal voice of the outsider: the facilitator of communication, the prosopopeia of maximal elimination
of noise, so as to hear the distant rumble of the world
and its demons in the midst of the ideal city of human
communication.

the elemental that faces ▮

One is called to the deathbed of a parent, and one, facing her, does not know what to say. Yet one has to say something.

The other has arrived at the limit—the limit of her life—when she can do nothing more. But she has yet this to do: to die. It is something she has to do, alone, and without any experience to appeal to, any means or resources. It is something she, nevertheless, has to do and will do well or badly, bravely or in collapse, resolutely or cowering. She has always known she will have to do this, has often thought of it, has often willed to die the one way or the other. For every time she did something bravely, or cowardly, it was an anticipation of this final confrontation. Aristotle, who wrote the first treatise in the West on rational ethics, listed courage first of all the virtues. It is not simply first on the list of equivalent virtues; it is the transcendental virtue, the condition for the possibility of all the virtues. For no one can be truthful, or magnanimous, or a friend, or even congenial in conversation, without courage. And every courage is an act done in

COURAGE

risk: <u>of one's reputation</u>, of one's job, of one's pos-
sessions, of one's life.

And you, called upon to be there when the other is
at the limit, and also at the origin, of the virtues, the
powers, that a life can have, find yourself at the limit
of the powers of language.

The nurses say, "I am so glad you have come!"
They know you can do, must do, something they cannot do—say something to the dying one. What can
one say? Anything one tries to say sounds vacuous
and absurd in one's mouth. It seems to you that the
problem is not simply that you do not have the skills
in speaking or that you cannot come up with the right
things to say because you have no experience in this
kind of situation, but that language itself does not
have the powers. There is not, in the words and the
combinatory possibilities of language, the power to
say what has to be said. Yet you have to be there, and
you have to say something. You have never been
more clear about anything. <u>There are those who do
not go</u>, to the bedside of the <u>dying one</u>, demoralized
by the terrible impotence of language to say anything.
It seems to them that, in their speechlessness, they
<u>are carried away already into the region of death</u> and
silence with the <u>other</u>. But if you somehow find the
courage to go, you are sure you have to be there and
have to say something. What is imperative is that you
be there and speak; what you say, in the end, hardly
matters. You end up saying anything—"It'll be alright,

Mom"—which you know is a stupid thing to say, even
an insult to her intelligence; she knows she is dying
and is more brave than you. She does not reproach
you for what you said; in the end it doesn't matter,
what was imperative was only that you say something,
anything. That your hand and your voice extend to her
in accompaniment to the nowhere she is drifting on
to, that the warmth and the tone of your voice come
to her as her own breath gives way, and that the light
of your eyes meet hers that are turned to where there
is nothing to see.

Everyone has known such a situation in which the
rift between the saying and the said opens up. A situation in which the saying, essential and imperative,
separates from the said, which somehow it no longer
orders and hardly requires.

In the rational community the other situation is the
normal one—that where what is said is the essential
and the saying inessential, that where what is imperative is only that whoever speaks, he say *this*.

Such is the situation when there is not simply, as in
every community, a common stock of observations,
maxims for action, and beliefs that are picked up from
others and passed on to others. The rational community produces, and is produced by, a common discourse in a much stronger sense. The insights of individuals are formulated in universal categories, such
that they are detached from the here-now index of the

one who first formulated them. Discourse sets out to supply a reason, that is, a more general formulation, an empirical law or a practical maxim, from which the observations and practices could be deduced. Establishing the empirical laws and practical principles distributes the insights of individuals to all. And then one sets out to supply a reason for the reason—the theory from which the laws and the principle from which the maxims could be deduced. These function to contest the validity of all statements that attest to simply individual observations and beliefs. The common discourse is not simply an accumulation of information and beliefs and maxims, but a rational system in which, ideally, everything that is said implicates the laws and theories of rational discourse. Then, when any rational agent speaks, he speaks as a representative of the common discourse. The law he formulates for his own understanding and practice legislates for the discourse of everyone, not because of any force or authority in his particular voice, but because the consistency and the coherence, the cogency, of the integrally one rational discourse imposes this statement.

When one goes to someone and asks him to speak, the imperative one lays on him is an imperative that he govern his speech with the imperative that regulates the common discourse and makes it rational. One goes to the doctor, the veterinarian, or the electrician, and one first assures oneself that he really speaks as a representative of the common discourse of rational culture. You ask, discreetly, a few questions: Doctor, what about this Japanese research I read about last week on pacemakers? Doctor, I just read this article about leukemia in cats and thought to come to ask you about my Persian, Simone, who seems to be ailing. Sir, I read about these new halogen lights; do you think they might be bad for the eyes, like the old fluorescent lights? What you are doing is checking out whether the person you are consulting might not be an eccentric—an electrician who does not keep up with knowledge in his field, a veterinarian who has his own theory about viruses that is incompatible with the general theories of today's biology. What there is to be said is in the literature available in the public libraries; one is only asking him to efficiently speak as the spokesman for what one could oneself discover in the literature.

There is something to be said. In principle, there is, in the common discourse of rational culture, something that has to be said, even if it is that the current state of science does not know the answer to the question you formulated—because the cancer is in the bile duct in the midst of a tangle of vital organs and cannot be removed by surgical incision with today's instruments, because testing for eye damage from halogen lamps will require a few years and they have just come into production last year.

When one speaks to the doctor, the veterinarian, or

the electrician, one speaks as a representative of the common rational discourse. One does not speak to the oncologist about the obscure intuition of fate in the individual circumstances of one's life one has long felt through only inward premonitions. One does not speak to one's veterinarian as a sentimental person who needs this cat as a child substitute. One might, to be sure, when outside in the hall making out the check, say to him, with a foolish smile, Doctor see what you can do with this cat, I love him like my own baby. The doctor will smile indulgently, and assure you he will do whatever science can do.

Speaking as a representative of the common discourse of rational culture is what we call serious speech. The seriousness in it is the weight of the rational imperative that determines what is to be said. Students demand of their teachers that they formulate, without eccentricities, the state of the art of their particular disciplines; one expects that what one learns in the sciences, in the humanities, and in the technologies will implicate the universal principles of the rational integration of knowledge. The vocalization of what has to be said in this particular voice, by this particular speaker, is inessential; the very saying is inessential, since what has to be said exists in the literature in the public libraries, or if not, is implicated already in the governing categories, theories, and methods of rational discourse.

We also indulge in eccentricities of discourse—our

doctor inquires after our golf game; our veterinarian smiles indulgently over our neurotic sentimentality. That is part, no doubt, of the pleasure of speaking in a community—the eccentric tropes we put in our professional rhetoric, the odd metaphors and far-fetched adjectives we attach to the operative nouns, the sexual metaphors we indulge in, with which we fabricate a public ego out of eccentricities. We do not take all that very seriously, nor do we take it to be imperative.

The limit-situation we invoked—when one of the community is departing from among us, when someone is at the end of his or her life—is also a situation in which we who go to their side, who *have to* go to their side, find ourselves at the limit of speech. This is not where the necessity of language ends in silence, but where it is no longer what has to be said that is the essential, and the saying and the one that says inessential: now you find you have to be there and have to speak. You have to say something—something that language cannot say, something that is not in the resources of common discourse to be able to say, and something that is, in the end, inessential. It is the saying that is imperative: your hand extended to the one who is departing, the light of your eyes meeting the eyes of the other that are turned to where there is nothing to see, and the warmth of your voice brought to her as her own breath gives way. This situation is not only the end of language—the last moment when

I care about you.

all we have to say to one another ends in the silence and death of the one to whom it has to be said and in the speechlessness and sobs of the one who has come to say something. It is also the beginning, the beginning of communication.

When we form that closed community that is the community of lovers, we often have the impression that our love does not need words. When people fall in love, they seem to have so much to say to one another, occupying the telephone long into fatigue of the hand to hold it and exhaustion of the ears to listen. One feels a compulsion to formulate the most trivial details of one's day, both as a kind of test—if she really will listen to all this, which nobody at the office would, she really must care for me—and as a rhetoric of seduction, an enterprise of making every detail of one's day into an adventure or an entertainment. But once their love is assured and sealed, they listen to music, watch television, or giggle nonsense. The talk that does go on is serious—she speaks of her professional worries and ambitions and he speaks of household repair problems and of his progress toward becoming a successful scientist or businessman, a representative of science or commerce. This serious talk seems outside their love; nobody thinks you really have to talk to your lover about laboratory or office problems at all.

It is when their love is dying that they feel something else. "You have to say something! About us! I don't want to hear any more about your boss or about what siding to put on the house! We have to talk about us!" You really do have to say something. You. And you have no idea what you can say. Even if you went through this before, when a love you then knew died. You find yourself saying anything—saying stupid things. It doesn't matter—you have to say something.

And then you get the idea that this had happened before—when you started. In a class it did not matter if it was you, or another student, that spoke in the seminar. What was essential was that the matter got discussed. The function of the seminar was that the professor formulate the problem out of the current state of the debate in political philosophy on the question of rights. The students were to formulate objections, alternatives, to the theses now being advanced. Sometimes you knew what was to be said, but let another student say it, because a seminar is not a place for you to be on an ego trip or become the professor's favorite. Then, with the adjacent student, some other relationship began to form—you found you were beginning to be lovers. Then, whenever you were together, you had to say something. What it was hardly mattered; what was essential was that you spoke, that the warmth of your voice accompany her in the uncharted zone of passion outside the classroom in which she was drifting, that the tone of your voice resonate in her languorous throat, and that the light of your eyes meet hers, unfocused on the task and the objectives, gazing toward the erotic darkness.

There are then two entries into communication—the one by which one depersonalizes one's visions and insights, formulates them in the terms of the common rational discourse, and speaks as a representative, a spokesperson, equivalent and interchangeable with others, of what has to be said. The other entry into communication is that in which you find it is you, you saying something, that is essential.

It is the last warm day of the autumn; the mother has to go to the park with her child. She forgets all the letters she has to write and the conference she has to prepare for this weekend; she forgets all her friends. She is totally absorbed in her task. She is seated at the pool, and a rainbow gleams across the fountain in the late-autumn sun. She is pointing to the rainbow in the pool. Her eyes are open wide and gleaming, jubilation trembling the coaxing lines of her mouth. She has to lead his eyes to it. This day. His eyes are too young to be able to see the rainbow in the sky. Next year it will be too late; he will be in kindergarten, with eyes already jaded by the electronic rainbows on television screens; he will have to look at books with pictures associated with the letters of the alphabet. She has to fix the focus of his eyes and teach him to see it. She has to teach him the word: rainbow. Rainbow in the fountain. He has to the learn the word and the wonder. She is wholly concentrated with the difficulty and the urgency of the task. She watches with anxiety and jubilation as the wonder fills his eyes, his eyes becoming wet with laughter, until she sees the rainbow on them.

What is it that speaks in these terminal and inaugural situations? Not the ego as a rational mind, as a representative of universal reason that possesses the a priori categories and the a priori forms of the rational organization of sensory impressions. What speaks is someone in his or her materiality as an earthling; one that breathes, sighs, and vocalizes in the rumble of the city and the murmurs of nature; one whose blood is warm with the warmth of the sun and the ardors of the night. One whose flesh is made of earth—dust that shall return to dust—who stands facing another with the support of the earth rising up in him or her; one whose face is made of light and shadow and whose eyes are made of light and tears.

We speak of aliens in our country, understanding by that people who do not share our language, who do not know the names we use to designate things and resources, who do not understand our laws and our principles of behavior and etiquette, and who therefore do not participate with us in building the work that is our common civilization. We also speak of the aliens that this work can make of those who participate in it; the alienation diagnosed by Marx is the dispossession of the products of one's labor, in which one had invested one's own properties—one's intelligence, one's imagination, one's skills, and the forces of one's muscles.

But there is also another alienation—an alienation from the elements. We go to places not only for the discourse that circulates there—the scientific community assembled there or the writers' colony—but for the sun, for the wide-open skies, for the tropical monsoons or for the dry sparkling air, for the desert or for the ocean. Sometimes when we go, we find ourselves immediately at home and resolve to stay there, even if we have no work there, know no one, and even do not know their language. But in most cases, we have to appeal to others to make ourselves at home. We appeal to the others to help us be at home in the desert, in the rain forest, in the tropics, in the tundra, and in the ocean. And in childhood, and in the strange nocturnal regions of the erotic, and in the shadow of death that advances.

This communication is other than and prior to, and it doubles up our communication as representatives of the rational community. It remains imperative when the other, with whom we had or not did not have a language in common, is departing. This communication that we all know has not been disengaged by our philosophies of language.

While classical epistemology endeavored to inventory the mental operations that identify, distinguish and relate objects, our philosophies of language have set out to show that these operations are performed in speech acts. The communication by which our own individual field of perception gets integrated with those of others is viewed as the means by which our minds get extended beyond the range of things that our own sense organs can reach, to the world of objects identifiable by all.

While classical epistemology took sensibility to record an unstructured flux of colors, lights, shadows, tones, and pressures, today the phenomenology of perception demonstrates that perception is, from the start, perception of things, structures, contours, paths, and landscapes. The phenomenology of perception isolates the structures and dynamics of perception, both from the physiology of neural conduction and from subsequent cognitive operations. Before we identify something with a word and a concept, it already takes form before our eyes and our exploring hands as a unit or a complex of units. You open a box someone has mailed you, and you see a thing but no have idea what it is or what it is called. You do not just experience retinal imprints on the separate rods and cones of your eyes and pressures in your own fingers. You perceive a thing with its own size and shape and observe its balance, symmetry, colors, solidity, and grain.

Each thing that rises in relief in a sensory field,

named or not, has a feedback effect on the subsequent patterns that form in perception. Anthropologist Colin Turnbull tells of taking a pygmy friend to the open savannah, where he saw a distant elephant as the size of a mosquito. Eyes that had learned to see in the depth of the rain forest, where the gaze in every direction had always been blocked within twenty feet by another tree trunk and where the skies had always been splintered by the forest canopy, were not able to see the small figure as a huge elephant at a remote distance.

But the system of objects we identify with our speech acts and relate with rational discourse also has a feedback effect on our perception. Others have directed our vision—with words. We are told how to look and given the names of what to look for. Someone who learns the language of meteorology sees the skies differently than before; someone who learns the names for things of an Amazonian hunting-and-gathering tribe sees the rain forest differently from the Western botanist and biologist.

The phenomenology of perception in recent decades has been much occupied with this feedback phenomenon between perception and the speech acts that identify objects with the taxonomy and grammar of a certain language. Paul Feyerabend argues not only that the languages of the different sciences, and those of different epochs of the same science, are incommensurable, untranslatable into one another, but also that the perceptions of the men of the Middle Ages, India, and the Amazon rain forest are incommensurable. Thomas Kuhn says that every new scientific revolution is not a new conceptual grid with which to view the same layout of nature and of the heavens; it is a Gestalt shift in which a new earth and a new heaven become visible.

These investigations move between the objective language of the rational community and the perception that has things as its objectives. The current phenomenology of perception takes it that when we look, our gaze is always, as Heidegger said, interested and preoccupied; we are on the lookout for something— some objective, tool, trap, or obstacle. The philosophy of language takes it that our natural, pre-scientific language functions to identify objects, instruments, paths, directions, or procedures, for one another. It envisions only that entry into communication that integrates the range of those things our own sense organs can reach, into the world of objects identifiable by all.

But if it is true that we do not live and act in the objective representation of the universe but in a perceived landscape for which the objective representation of the universe is a map, this perceived landscape is not simply a multiplicity of discrete things distributed at eye's reach. The things we can distinguish and identify in perception are themselves laid out in a clearing full of light, in a region of warmth and an at-

mosphere in which we can move and therefore explore perceptually, and over a ground that does not
extend as another object but as a dimension of support. These nonthings in which things form are what
Emmanuel Levinas has thematized as _the elemental._
The phenomenology of perception requires a phenomenology of sensibility—not an understanding of
the physiological organs and psychophysiological
channels which capture sensations, information-bits,
but a recognition of the sensuous element sensibility
knows and in which perception establishes some directions and positions some things.

We do not relate to the light, the earth, the air, and
the warmth only with our individual sensibility and
sensuality. We communicate to one another the light
our eyes know, the ground that sustains our postures,
and the air and the warmth with which we speak. We
face one another as condensations of earth, light, air,
and warmth and orient one another in the elemental
in a primary communication. We appeal to the others
to help us be at home in the alien elements into which
we stray: in the drifting and nameless light and
warmth of infancy, in the nocturnal depths of the
erotic, and in the domain of dying where rational discourse has no longer anything to say. The philosophy
of language which determines how things perceived
are said and how the saying communicates, requires a
phenomenology of the saying that occurs when the

one faces the other with the light and warmth and carnal substance of his or her face.

The Pythagorean world of numbers, the Platonic world of forms, and the modern scientific universe of formulas are laid out like maps over the implements and obstacles stationed along the roads of the city and the halls of the constructions of culture, and over the landscape of things at rest, animals roving, plants proliferating, and minerals shifting in the contours of the earth. But the space where the things are encountered is not suspended in the network of geometric dimensions or in the void. It extends in the light, in the warmth, in the atmosphere, and in a clearing stabilized on the supporting element of earth. Light is not, like a thing, explorable from different angles and perspectives; it offers no sides, and it is not approached like we approach the surfaces it illuminates. We find ourselves in the light. It is not a substance, supporting and known through its properties; it is luminosity, not a property of any thing, a free-floating adjective. Warmth is not something we perceive from a distance and apprehend; we find it by immersion. Ground is not, save for astronauts and for the imagination of astronomers, the planet, that is, a spherical substance that can be viewed from the distance once one no longer feels its support. For us earthlings, the ground is pure depth of support, supported by nothing,

which supports all things in their places. We know it
from within, in the stability of our own axis of posture. The night is not a black surface that stops our
sight on the surfaces of our own retinas; our look
goes out into the night, which is vast; the night invades, it is within as well as without. The elemental
does not extend, like a landscape of things, in horizons which show perception the distant and the future; its presence is full, there by incessant oncoming
and without a future we apprehend or project, in gratuitous abundance. The elemental is immemorial; the
vibrancy of the light about us dissolves all traces of its
own past forms, and the supporting sustenance of the
ground is felt present within the stability and agility of
our posture which does not retain residues of past
support.

Things are found in the elemental. Substances that
have contours that contain their properties, they can
be apprehended, detached, possessed. One identifies
oneself and maintains one's own identity in the midst
of things. The elemental which extends no horizons
of objectives, which passes into no stock that can be
recalled, does not lend itself to appropriation. One
cannot make oneself something separate and consoli-
date oneself by appropriating the light, by making private property and depriving others of the atmosphere,
by monopolizing the warmth, by expropriating the
things distributed over the ground of their support.
The light that invades the eyes depersonalizes and the

anonymity of light illuminates in one's eyes; one sees as eyes of flesh see. The forest murmurs and the rumble of the city invade one's ears that hear as hearing hears. The ground that rises up into one's posture depersonalizes; one stands as trees stand, one walks as terrestrial life walks, and one rests as terrestrial life rests, and as rocks and sands rest.

The elemental is not a multiplicity of discrete things successively perceived in their places from vantage points and collated; it is not sensed by a perception which identifies surface patterns. The elemental is sensed in a pure sense of depth, not by an intentional direction of the viewing eye and the grasping hand aiming at objectives, but by a movement of involution. The movement that senses the elemental is not the movement of need or want, the movement of an emptiness that seeks, in the distance, a content; it is a movement of immersion in a plenum. The sense of the elemental senses itself affected with, filled with, and nourished by the elemental in a sensuous accord which the word *enjoyment* designates. The light bathes the eyes as soon as they open and buoys up the movement of sight toward the surfaces and contours of things it illuminates. It does not spread a screen of color before the sight; its own color dissolves to leave the colors of the things it illuminates glow with their own phosphorescence. But it is not neutral or pure transparency; the enjoyment in seeing senses the hue and the sparkle and vibrancy of the light. The eyes that see with the light enjoy seeing; the vitality caressed and sustained by the warmth of the day enjoys being warmed; the gait sustained by the ground enjoys walking and enjoys wandering aimlessly in the sustaining region of the terrestrial. The lungs that breathe in the air enjoy savoring the good air. The ears do not only harken to the signals and the threats; they enjoy hearing the forest murmurs and the rumble of the city. The home is not only a closed vault full of implements and stocked to satisfy needs; it is a zone of tranquility and warmth and a precinct of intimacy recessed from the uncharted expanses of the alien, recognized in enjoyment. And we enjoy enjoying our homes.

We do not live by labor alone or by bread alone. Life is not a succession of initiatives driven by need and want and aiming at objectives. Life is not the recurrence of need and satisfaction, eating and getting hungry again and drinking and getting thirsty again, in an enterprise that is gradually losing its reserve, in an anxiety repeatedly postponing death. Life is enjoyment. We live in light, in warmth, in liquidity, in radiance, in the rumble of sonority and the music of the spheres, in the intimacy of home and homeland and in the immensities of the exotic.

The sensuous involution in the elemental makes one's eyes luminous, one's hands warm, one's posture supportive, one's voice voluble and spiritual and one's face ardent. In the involution of enjoyment is generated the gratuitous and excess energies that seek release in exultation. Enjoyment is freedom; in the enjoyment of the radiance of the spring day and the warmth of the ground, we forget our cares, our cravings, and our objectives; we forget our losses and our compensations and we let go of what holds us. Every enjoyment is a death: a dying we know, not as the Heideggerian anxiety knows it—being hurled from being into nothingness—and not as pain knows it—a being mired in oneself and backed up into oneself by the passage into passivity—but as dissolution into the beginningless, endless, and fathomless plenum of the elemental.

It is before the face of another that our enjoyment becomes our own. Our own to give.

To see the other as another sentient agent is to see his postures and movements directed to a range of implements and obstacles about him. To see the other is to see her place as a place I could occupy and the things about her as harboring possibilities that are open to my skills and initiatives. It is to see the other as another one like I am, equivalent to and inter-changeable with me. It is the sense of the death awaiting me that circumscribes the range of possibili-ties ahead of me. To see the other as one who has his own tasks and potentialities is to sense another death circumscribing the field of possibilities ahead of him.

But the other turns to me, empty-handed, from across that wall of death. She appeals to the skills and resources of my hands. Heidegger calls inauthentic, inauthentifying, the solicitude with which I substitute my skills for his and take over his tasks for him. What the other asks is not for this disburdening, this displacement from her own tasks. She asks of my hands the diagram of the operations her hands seek to perform, and he asks the assistance of my forces, lest his be wanting. But he or she appeals first for terrestrial support, the support that my stand on the earth has to give. Robinson Crusoe, in Michel Tournier's novel *Friday*, writes, "I know now that the very earth beneath my feet needs to be trodden by feet other than mine if I am to be sure of its substance." Peter Mathiessen asks that men of the Himalayas ground him on this mountain where he has come to study the snow leopard; Gertrud Trun asks of the people of the Lacandone rain forest that they ground her in Chiapas where she has come to photograph the butterflies and the orchids of the forests; George Abramson asks of the men of Africa that they ground him in the savannah where he has come to return the lions to liberty; Ché Guevara asks of the men of the Bolivian Andes that they ground him in the rain forests where he has come to combat the dictator. The fatigue, the vertigo, and the homelessness in his or her body appeals for the force of terrestrial support from those whose earthbound bodies have the sense of this earth and this terrain to give. The other turns to the terrestrial support in my stand; if, while extending my skills to her tasks, I do not offer this support to her, she will prefer to work out the ways and the operations on her own, by trial and error.

The hand of the other extended to mine seeks not only the skills in my hand, which is an instrument among others available for his or her own tasks; in the clasped handshake with which we greet one another and set out each to his or her own tasks, each one seeks the warmth of the hand of another—the elemental warmth in which vitality is immersed.

The other, whom I see as a focus of vision open to the surfaces and contours of the landscape open to me too—a different vision that surveys the range of a landscape of possibilities whose relief the black wall of his or her own death circumscribes about him or her—looks at me with the nakedness and vulnerability of his or her eyes. His or her look appeals to the vision in my eyes. But not only for the foresight and hindsight that can chart his or her way for him or her: he or she appeals first for light. In solitude, Robinson Crusoe learns the frightening nakedness of his eyes. He realizes that the eyes of others had extended beyond the narrow radius of things he sees, fields of things already seen or being seen by us; alien eyes extend the map of the visible. His solitude means that these other lights are gone and black night narrows the visible to what he himself actually sees. His eyes cease to function as a light source that circulates among objects that were visible before he came upon them and remain visible on the margin of what he now sees. The colors and the shadows invade his eyes, like opacities inhering in them which the eye can no longer situate outside. His sight becomes a tube where a fragment of the visible abruptly blazes, like a blow struck without warning. When other eyes were there, they kept the light luminous beyond the narrow radius of what is actually visible to him.

When someone's eyes turn to me, it is other light sources they seek, glowing in the light, to extend the depth of light in which he or she circulates. Sometimes, to be sure, the other looks to me to receive from me the image of what my eyes have seen; the other I meet on the Himalayan trek asks of me if I have seen the path to the grand visions that eyes are made to see. But the other's look does not look to my eyes to see there the surfaces and contours of the landscape upon which I hold my look. It first seeks the vivacity and radiance of the light in my eyes, and it seeks the shadows and the darkness my eyes harbor with care. If it does not find them, if it finds only the look of a surveyor recording the topography, it will prefer to look on its own for the radiance and the twilights of the world.

The other turns to me and speaks; he or she asks something of me. Her words, which I understand because they are the words of my own tongue, ask for information and indications. They ask for a response that will be responsible, will give reasons for its reasons and will be a commitment to answer for what it answers. But they first greet me with an appeal for responsiveness. His words seek out a voice voluble and spiritual, whose orders, coherence, and direction are interrupted, of itself, by hesitations, redundancies, and silences, questioning him by questioning itself. In the very explanation and instruction the other seeks, he or she seeks his or her own voice in my silences and my questions. If my voice is not responsive to this quest, he or she will seek in books the answers to his or her perplexities.

The face of the other is a surface upon which the axes and directions of his posture and the intentions of his movements are exposed to me. The face of the other is a surface upon which the forms of her comprehension are expressed to me. The face of the other is a surface of suffering, upon which her sensitivity and susceptibility and her vulnerability and mortality are exposed to me. This surface is made of light and shadows, of carbon compounds, earth; his eyes glisten and move with the liquidity of the elemental; her voice is made of air and warmth. The face of the other is a surface of the elemental—the place where the elemental addresses, appeals and requires, the involution in enjoyment which makes one's own eyes luminous, one's hands warm, one's posture supportive, one's voice voluble and spiritual, and one's face ardent. The face of the other is the place where the elemental surfaces to make demands on the elemental resources in which the enjoyment of my life is immersed.

What the face of the other asks for is not the inauthentic and inauthentifying solicitude with which I substitute my skills for his, take over her tasks for her, view the forms and the landscape for him, formulate the answers to the questions in her stead. He does not seek his or her contentment in the content that will satisfy his needs and wants, which I can supply from my place and my resources and with my skills— the contentment which, when he has been displaced by me and disburdened of his own tasks, will leave him only the weight and death of the inorganic. In seeking the support of my upright stand on the earth, the agile luminousness that shines in my eyes, the warmth in my hands, the ardor in my face, and the spirituality in my breath, the other seeks the pleasure that is enjoyment in, involution and the dying in, the elemental. The other seeks the contact and the accompaniment.

carrion body carrion utterance ▪

*E*very discourse among interlocutors is a struggle against outsiders, those who emit interference and equivocation, who have an interest in that the communication not take place. But in the measure that communication does take place and that statements are established as true, it designates outsiders as not making sense, as mystified, mad, or brutish, and it delivers them over to violence.

What can be true is a statement that can be integrated into the common discourse. Statements can be true, and meaningful, only in the discourse of an established community that determines what could count as observations, what degrees of accuracy in recording observations are possible, how the words of common language are restricted and refined for different kinds of cognition and for practical or technological uses, and what could count as an argument. Truth requires a community with institutions that set up and fund exploration, research, and laboratories to gather information and observations according to community standards of accuracy and repeatability;

no such thing as universal truth?

institutions that determine the grammatical and rhetorical forms in which theoretical or technological research is to be reported, and its conclusions formulated; and institutions that establish what counts as argument and what counts as evidence in logic, physics, history, literary criticism or Biblical scholarship, economics, penology, jurisprudence, and military strategy. Truth requires institutions that select researchers, teach them the paradigms of successful research, and train them to repeat and apply that research to batches of other material selected by institutional criteria; it requires institutions that certify and evaluate their researchers and technicians. It requires institutions that select what research is to be published and how it is to be judged. All these institutions recruit and train their members and are funded and controlled by institutions that regulate the command posts by which the established community monopolizes and elaborates its power.

Aristotle has delegated to us the notion that truth is a property of judgments, a characteristic—of adequation—that inheres in a statement as its own property. But the determination of truth is not at all the work of a solitary thinker who simply inspects the intrinsic properties of statements taken one by one. Every truth is an established truth, the truth of a certain institution or institutional complex.

And every institution institutes or establishes a truth. Whenever a community is founded and whenever the constitution and laws and boundaries and command posts of a state are founded, the truth for that community is instituted.

A discourse established as true functions both indicatively, as information and advance representation of things and situations, and vocatively and imperatively, as an utterance calling upon and summoning before it the presence of individuals. It summons them bodily.

institution / community ↓ TRUTH

True discourse is discourse which is based on bodily sensations; it records what individuals have seen and heard, what their body powers can vouch for. But the sensibleness, the sanity, of discourse in the community is independent of the bodies of individuals; one verifies the consistency and coherence, the rationality, and the verifiability of that discourse without considering the body's health or sanity, at all. The ability to integrate statements about what one has seen and heard into the body of established truth is governed not by biological or psychophysiological, but by rational, logical, and scientific laws: that is, institutional criteria.

The individual who is subjected to the institutional imperative to say what he sees and experiences must say it in statements subjected to the contestation and verification of others of the community. He must formulate his living insights and experiences in the established concepts of the language—in forms that are not his own, but are the forms of anyone. His most inti-

he becomes responsible for his explanation

mate and living impulses and insights lose their individuality in being formulated; his thoughts are put in the coffers of words that preserve them like tombs preserve, such that later, when he hears or reads his own thoughts, he finds in the words only what anyone else finds; he no longer finds the lithe and virgin fires of his own inner life. When he speaks, he speaks as one in whose statement the logic, theories, and cognitive methods of his culture are implicated; he speaks as a representative, equivalent and interchangeable with another, of the established truth. All the ephemeral insights of his sentient body are continued, maintained, or lost in the anonymous body of discourse of the instituted science and culture.

In savage societies, language as utterance separates from and prevails over language as statement of information established as truth. What Montaigne identified as the word of honor separates from the informative word.[1] The savage is an exposed body, resolute and proud in the force with which he advances naked into the rain forests and the savannah. The bodies of others are viewed directly in their strength and speed, sensitivity and clairvoyance, and audacity and endurance—individual attributes which are not observed and recorded in inevitably common categories, but experienced and tested in contention with them. The

1. Montaigne, "On Cannibals."

savage advances unto the bodies of others, warriors proudly arrayed with the plumes of eagles and the tusks of wild boars, to wage a contest of courage and honor with them. Their bodies are not armed to defend an established institution; their outcries do not proclaim an established truth. Their shouts addressed individually to warriors are performative words with which the savage commits himself, words addressed to the arms and the deadly force of the other, words in which he stands and stakes his life. As he triumphs or falls, he intones a cry of glory, the cry of eagles or lions, or utters a last cry of insubmission and defiance.

An established discourse summons the individuals it informs, directing them to the things and situations it formulates. But an established discourse can also exclude the individuals it summons from the things and situations it determines.

The philosopher is one who speaks in the midst of an established culture, but finds that the body of statements established in that culture weaken or disintegrate under the effect of skeptical doubt. In a tactical alliance with skeptics, he finds his vocation and his dignity in separating himself from the body of statements, not by making new observations to be accounted for alongside the established ones, but by revealing inconsistencies and incoherences in the established canons which determine what can count as observations, what levels of accuracy in determining observations are possible, in what terms and in what kinds of formulation the observations are to be reported, and what can count as argument in the diverse cognitive disciplines and practical spheres. The established discourse ceases to function, for the philosopher, as a determination of things and situations in which he lives his life and now functions as an utterance, calling upon and requiring the philosopher in person. The philosopher works not to disestablish the truth, but to establish the truth more securely.

The psychotic, the pariah, and the mystic find themselves not informed by the established discourse, not directed to the things and situations it formulates, and not summoned to contribute to its establishment. This could be nowise a problem about the established discourse functioning as statements; it could well be that one could find oneself excluded by the body of statements whose veracity is nowise in question, statements whose veracity one has no doubts about. Statements that are firm, established, and acknowledged as reliable and veridical, address to these individuals but one utterance, "You are incapable of truth!" The pariah, the mystic, and the psychotic know this utterance in the suffering and torment of their bodies. What is designated as a mind in decomposition in a brutish body is not simply an entity excluded from the objects that the established body of statements identifies and recognizes; it is tortured by the institutions that establish the truth.

cruelty /
torture
not
premeditated
(usually)

When the violence called up by an aggressive blow is not discharged in a counter-blow, its forces are accumulated and exasperated in the time that elapses before it finds its revenge. A group may wreck extreme violence upon someone against whom it has long been accumulating suspicions and grievances. But it is doubtful that torture, when it enters into the practices of institutions, does so as a result of the confluence of a number of violent and vindictive individuals. Would not the solitary monster be produced, not by an atavist regression to the instincts of beasts of prey, but by a condensation in him of the methods of violence elaborated in institutions? It seems clear that confirmed rapists act not out of the raw sex drive stripped of social control, but out of the contraction in them of the institutional imagoes and practices of the millennial patriarchical society. The one that gouges out the eyes of his victim has not regressed to the presocialized instincts of apes but has ascended to the ranks of the Ottoman Janissaries and the agents of the Roman Inquisition. To emerge and be maintained, torture presupposes not certain instincts but certain institutions.

systems
theory

desire & power

) ☜

It is as fanatics, subversives, savages, and insane—individuals whose basic antisocial act consists in not making sense—that offenders are not simply coerced into obedience or restitution, but are tortured. Torture is instituted where there is a totalitarian power, but also a certain kind of established discourse.

ALPHONSO LINGIS

Michel Foucault has shown how the practice of torture instituted in the ancien régime in Europe ensued
from the contact of the body of the offender with the
established truth incarnated in the doubly transcendentalized body of the monarch.[2] The body of the
monarch did not simply symbolize the social order
but materialized the body of the State, and was invested with power by divine right as an incarnation of
the resurrected body of Christ the King who is the
Way and the Truth and the Life. Every crime that occupied royal justice was a crime of lèse-majesté. Many
social offenses were not covered by the king's justice
at all—economic crimes which were penalized by the
guilds and by the town officials, aggressions and mur-
ders which were avenged by the community or the
family who suffered the aggression, and transgres-
sions of canon law which were penalized by the ecclesiastical courts. When the agents of the king rode into
a town to seek out a criminal and bring him to justice,
he was treated as one who had offended the very person of the king—more exactly, assaulted the body of
the king. The body of the king was the substance that
materialized the coherence and consistency of the
truth established in the heavens and instituted in the
structure of the State. This absolutization of the body
of the monarch made intelligible the subjecting of the

2. Michel Foucault, *Discipline and Punish*, trans. Alan Sheridan
(New York: Vintage. 1979); Ernst Kantorowicz, *The King's Two Bodies* (Princeton: Princeton University Press, 1957).

enemy of the king to aggression without limit: pour-
ing boiling oil down his throat, gouging out his eyes,
branding and quartering his body, and burning it at
the stake. The stake piled with faggots was set up in
the public square, and all the king's subjects were
summoned to attend this theater where the criminal
was suspended between the heavens and the flames
of hell already rising up to consume him. The tortured
body of the king's enemy was made into the substance upon which the sacredness of the sovereign
body of the king was emblazoned.

Enlightenment Europe was to send to the guillotine
the bodies of its monarchs and the truth incarnated in
them. Scientifico-technological rationality, not relative
to any realm or dynasty and extending its domain over
all regional discourses that invoke sacred or ancestral
authority whose seriousness and consistency it adjudi-
cates, will be absolutized across the planet. Its truths
are established with technological, pedagogical, economic, and political institutions. Universities and research institutes represent themselves as the institutions in which the criteria for common truth is
established; in fact, they submit their projects and
curricula to parliaments for implementation. Parliaments represent themselves as forums where the insights of representative individuals are freely elaborated and integrated with one another in provisional
syntheses; in fact, parliaments function as board-
rooms where the interests of the most powerful insti-

tutions of the disciplinary archipelago are coordinated and transcendentalized as law. Parliament replaces the body of the king as the body in which the coherence and consistency of every institution—economic, multinational-corporate, juridical, industrial, educational, scientific, and religious—is represented, and their integration in the national and also international order is elaborated.

The aliens on other continents, encountered as the European Enlightenment extended its scientifico-technological and political institutions across the planet, were conceptualized by Hegel, as by Plato, as barbarians, animals without language, living, according to Hegel, in a tropical and torpid hypnogogic state of reverie. Animals with different bodies, they were insensitive, according to Nietzsche, to the pain of the misery and whips to which the rational community subjects them. But the ultimate and essential term with which they were designated by the Enlightenment is *cannibal*. The term fixed the most extreme repugnance with which the Enlightenment could view savages, those torpid dreamers who had no self and no self-consciousness: their bodies were, in fact, not their own, but composed out of the corpses of others, carrion themselves. Cannibalism was alleged everywhere the European conquistadors went, and tortured and enslaved: in the Caribbean; among the Aztecs, the Mayas, the Incas; across Africa; and in Polynesia. On the gibbets of the European absolute monarchy,

the bodies of Europeans confessed that they had de-
livered themselves over to the Prince of Darkness, and
the torture emblazoned on them the divine right of
the body of the king. In the outer realms where the
European power extended its Enlightenment, the torture of the Caribs, Amerindians, Africans, Asians, and
Polynesians forced them to confess to being cannibals
and forced from them the utterances of carrion
bodies. *— not true.*

Today, torture is more widespread than ever. Torture does not subsist only in archaic and pariah en-
claves of autocracy, but it ravages especially in the cli-
ent states[3] of the advanced powers that proclaim
allegiance to the established scientifico-technological
rationality and represent themselves as representational democracies. Torture, today, is no longer con-
ducted in the public square before the whole community, nor before the television cameras, but in secret
dungeons by covert-action commandos in the outer
provinces of the global scientifico-technological empire, where the voices of its victims, their screams and
their sobs, are lost in the night and the fog. Its victims
are not identified as sacrilegious regicides but as subversives, fanatics, maniacs, and terrorists.

The torturer works to tear away at the victim's body
and prove to him that he is a terrorist and that what

3. El Salvador, Peru, Kuwait, Kenya, Angola . . .

he believed in is aberration and delusion. The instruments and techniques of torture do have the power
to render a body incapable and brutish, by tearing
away at its integrity and proving it cowardly and cra-
ven. The most courageous militants make sure they
carry, at all times, vials of cyanide to bite open. For
torture is not just a contest of wills, between torturer
and captive; it is armed with a technology that can
reduce the will to impotent ferocity in a mass of ob-
scene members and organs.

The torturer demands of the victim that as his body
is being reduced to a mass of pain and gore, he say
something—that he confess. Confess what? Not that
the instituted regime, policy, and doctrine is true. The
established body of statements, determined by the established ways things and situations are observed, by
the established terms and formulations with which
they are reported, and by the established ways reports
and possibilities are argued, are true because they determine things and situations and not because they
are continually substantiated by the individuals to
whom they are offered. The institution does not conceive of the one being tortured, or any individual subject, as one who must contribute to its truth, who has
a part to play in the constitution of truth, and who has
a part to play also in the structure of power, which
would construct and be constructed out of the truth
to which all contribute. Were it to conceive of the individual that way, then that would amount to conceiv-

ing of itself as not yet being true or being true only contingent on the assent of a multiplicity of knowing and acting subjects. The established scientifico-technological truth is manifested in the planetary nature it coerces into obedience and does not, like the monarchical order, require the theater of the gibbet for its proclamation. It tortures in the night and fog. If it is established as the institution of truth and justice, then all it asks, and all it can ask, of the individual is that he confess; that is, bear witness to it and represent its truth in his body by confessing himself incapable of truth. The one being tortured is not being asked to declare true what he knows to be false. The torturer demands that he confess that he is incapable of making sense, that his body is incapable of lucidity and discernment, that it is nothing but corruption and putrefaction. Not only that he does not have a mind capable of contributing to or verifying the truth of the institution, but that he does not have a body capable of holding together. The utterance the institution demands to hear from the individual is that he confesses to being filth and shit—that he is already the carrion the torture is making of him.

The one that tortures is not an agent that maintains the institution and contributes to its truth; he is one outside of public view, one who works in the dungeons and the night, who knows himself to be scum and refuse.

The one that has confessed can then be incinerated,

having already acknowledged that he is nothing but rotting flesh. Or else he can then be used by the institution for any purpose, such as the torture of others, for example. Whatever will be done through his hands will be covered over with the truth and justice of the institution, while he knows and acknowledges to himself that he is nothing but decomposition and shit.

The body of the victim, reduced to corruption, is still the locus where something resists. The torture victim who finds a resistance in himself, even in the degradation to which he is subjected, does not find this resistance in his character or his will; militants carry vials of cyanide because they know that torturers can crush all character and break any will. What resists in oneself are the comrades who are not corrupt like oneself, the anger and suffering that is born and reborn with every generation of repression, the struggle which did not depend on oneself and will survive one.[4] What resists in the body of the captive, from whom the torturer demands a confession, is an utterance, identified by the torture victim as the utterance of comrades in the cause that does not depend on one, the mute utterance of the suffering from which one could no longer protect the others, and of their anger, from which one could not expect anything.

The torture victim hears, as an utterance addressed

4. Michel de Certeau, *Heterologies,* trans. Brian Massumi (Minneapolis: University of Minnesota Press, 1986), p. 43.

to him, the silence of his comrades and of his cause. What is asked of him by this utterance is that he sacrifice his body to the word and that he disincarnate himself in the torture that reduces his body to carrion, in order to rise again as the word and the truth. If his cause prevails, it will establish itself and establish its truth. His pain, his decomposition, and his corpse will become an emblem and a glorious memory and will be reinscribed in the truth of the new order.

But if his comrades and his cause do not prevail? He knows they may not, and very often he knows they will not. Honor requires that he die without confession. That he die uttering a word of honor in the face of his captors and torturers. Honor requires that he proclaim his community with those with whom no one has anything in common: with the mystics and the terrorists and the savages that prowl on the outer deserts of the established truth of civilization.

This does not mean that a savage community remembers the valor of the fallen one through remembering his utterance, and that a savage community outside of every institution exists because there is a common memory of those valorous in defeat.

Those devoted to establishing the truth are sure that the utterances of the tortured, the subversives, the mystics, the insane, and the savages, are addressed to them. The philosopher, from his distance from the established truth, hears these utterances made across another distance as alien, alienated, forms of skepticism addressed to the body of discourse established as true. The psychoanalyst is sure that all the rhetoric of the patient's dreams, actes manqués, gestures, psychosomatic symptoms, and slips of the tongue are addressed to him as a doctor and father, a representative of the institution and of the established truth. His therapy is an enterprise of bringing the silence and autistic discourse of the patient into the formulations of communicable and common truth; his science enlarges the established truth by integrating into it the private myth of the insane. Postmodern psychoanalysis aims, as Foucault wrote, at making the extravagances of Hölderlin, Nerval, Nietzsche, and Artaud part of *our* discourse and a project advancing toward the day when "everything that we experience today in the mode of the limit, or of strangeness, or of the unbearable will have joined again with the serenity of the positive."[5] Religion hears the utterances that come from the physical torments suffered by the mystics as information for its ecclesiastical logos. The contemporary enlightenment aims, as Merleau-Ponty wrote, at an enlarged conception of sense, by incorporating the nonsense of the insane, the mystics, the cannibals, and the screams of the torture victims.

But the *other* that the carrion utterance of the torture victim, the psychotic, the mystic, and the terrorist

5. "La folie, l'absence d'oeuvre," *La table ronde*, May 1964.

addresses is not only the men of the institution. His utterance is not destined only to the establishment of the truth that tortures him; it is even not only destined to the savages outside of all institutions. The screams and oaths of the *Grundsprache*, the fundamental language, of Daniel Paul Schreber, and his grimaces, contortions, and catatonia are not only so many gestures of a rhetoric his body addresses to the psychiatrist. It is not only addressed to the human community, but to that which is other than the human community: the celestial birds, the rays of the sun that seismically burn and electrify him, the insects, frogs, and rats, and the rocks and the empty skies.[6]

"Ockham, the modernist, the Inceptor as he was called," Michel de Certeau writes, "pioneered the notion, which gained general currency in theologians' opinion, that divine power is foreign to any theological or metaphysical system of rationality. One day, God may will salvation and, the next, the annihilation of an entire nation. Our reason has no stable connection with his decisions."[7] The mystic hears the utterance of this God in the torture he knows in his body. His carrion utterance is addressed to the God to whom one is no use and to whom one could not offer one's services.

6. See Alphonso Lingis, "The Din of the Celestial Birds," in David B. Allison, Prado de Oliveira, Mark S. Roberts, and Allen S. Weiss, *Psychosis and Sexual Identity: Toward a Post-Analytic View of the Schreber Case* (Albany: State University of New York Press, 1988), pp. 130–44.

7. Michel de Certeau, *Heterologies*, p. 108.

One day parliaments may will the salvation and, the next, the extermination of entire peoples; in the torment of the Quechua Indians, the Amazonian peoples, the Papuans, the Cambodians, and the Palestinians, no stable connection with the institutions of the scientifico-technological world order can be made. In the secret dungeons of covert-action commandos in the outer provinces of the global scientifico-technological empire, the torture victims do not face the institution and their voices, their screams and their sobs, are not recorded by the institution. In the resistance in his body, the torture victim hears the screams of his tortured comrades and hears the silence of the suffering from which one could no longer protect the others, and of their anger, from which one could not expect anything. He hears the grinding of the technological machinery of torture in the empty skies into which his screams and his sobs are lost, in the cement of the dungeon walls into which they are muffled, in the rock strata of the silent planet into which they sink. Yet a carrion utterance resounds in that night and fog. Something of the clamor of toads over the swamps stinking with the effluvia dripping out of the pipes of industry and of the swarming of centipedes and rats over the ruins, stirs in him and reverberates in the resistance in him.

community in death ▮▮▮

*W*e call society the forms of commitment, sealed in
the handshake that marks an agreement, in which we
associate in the exchange of messages, resources, and
services. In these exchanges, the common discourse
of science and culture can form and collective works
be undertaken in which we communicate in the possession and production of something in common.

Something else is communicated in the handshake
that associates after the agreement is conceived and
assented to: the recognition of kinship. Our language, which identifies things and persons with generic terms and formulates general imperatives for individuals, is the language of our bodies whose kinship
we recognize. In kinship, the genus is re-presented,
corporeally reduplicated, in the reproduction of individuals. The common words, with which we designate
the resources we separately know and the project we
separately understand, find their warrant in the com-
monality of the genus incarnated in our bodies. In the
recognition of kinship, the mutual commitment to the
common language and the reciprocal commitments in
the forms of exchange are confirmed. The monster is

one who, in his acts, impugns the claim of the genus in other individuals and in his own organism. With the handshake that seals an agreement, each one renounces the monster in the individuality of his or her body and its concupiscences.

It is not through seeing "family resemblances" that one recognizes kinship; the recognition of kinship is a recognition of obligation. The prodigal son that returns to his family knowing that he will be received demonstrates that when every trust, every commitment, and all communication in the civilized language that ceaselessly formulates the norms are broken, being-of-the-family subsists as the ground, in the generic structure of our bodies, of the imperative that imposes effective recognition. One's people are those of one's own lineage, and also possible spouses with whom one's lineage can be reproduced and people who will care for one's offspring as their own, if one dies. Being of the clan, being of the same people, or even being North American or of the white race is recognized in a recognition of obligation. This the traveler knows, who will not turn away (or will not turn away indifferently) from the appeal for assistance of someone, with whom he may have no interests or tastes in common, but who, like himself, is a Chicano in Pennsylvania, a North American in the Peruvian Andes, or a white man in the Sahel.

In the association in the exchange of messages, resources, and services, where each one confronts the others with his own insight and power, there is recognition of kinship which becomes effective as, in the exchanges contracted, each augments the other as he augments himself. When individuals associate, they identify those outside their agreements as barbarians and monsters; the effective recognition of common humanity extends as the exchange of messages, resources, and services with outsiders establishes an agreement with reciprocal commitments.

Beyond the effective recognition of kinship in the forms of society is something else: the brotherhood of individuals who possess or produce nothing in common, individuals destitute in their mortality. It is real in the exchange not of insights, directions, and resources but of the life of different individuals. The one becomes the brother of the other when he puts himself wholly in the place of the death that gapes open for the other.

To catch sight, beyond kinship, of this community in death, we should have to find ourselves, or put ourselves through imagination, in a situation at the farthest limits from kinship—in a situation in which one finds oneself in a country with which one's own is at war, among foreigners bound in a religion that one cannot believe or which excludes one, with whom one is engaged in no kind of productive or commercial dealings, who owe one nothing, who do not understand a word of one's language, who are far from one in age (for even being of the same age-group is a commitment)—and on whom one finds oneself completely dependent, for one's very life.

One night, sick for weeks in a hut in Mahabali-puram in the south of India, I woke out of the fevered stupor of days to find that the paralysis that had incapacitated my arms was working its way into my chest. I stumbled out into the starless darkness of the heavy monsoon night. On the shore, gasping for air, I felt someone grasp my arm. He was naked, save for a threadbare loincloth, and all I could understand was that he was from Nepal. How he had come here, to the far south of the Indian subcontinent—farther by far than I who, equipped with credit card, could come here from my home in a day by jet plane—I had no way of learning from him. He seemed to have nothing, sleeping on the sands, alone. He engaged in a long conversation, unintelligible to me, with a fisherman awakened from a hut at the edge of the jungle and finally loaded me in an outrigger canoe to take me, I knew without understanding any of his words, through the monsoon seas to the hospital in Madras sixty-five miles away. My fevered eyes contemplated his silent and expressionless face, from time to time illuminated by the distant flashes of lightning as he labored in the canoe, and it was completely clear to me that should the storm become violent, he would not hesitate to save me, at the risk of his own life.

We disembarked at a fishing port, where he put me

first on a rickshaw and then on a bus for Madras, and then he disappeared without a word or glance at me. He surely had no address but the sands; I would never see him again. I shall not cease seeing what it means to come to be bound with a bond that can never be broken or forgotten, what it means to become a brother.

How indecent to speak of such things in the anonymous irresponsibility of a writing he cannot read and a tongue he cannot understand!

We know ourselves in our mortality.

We act in a world that extends as an array of possibilities; the world we come to know through our initiatives is a field of sustenance, resources, implements, paths, dangers, and shelters. We apprehend the possibilities of the world with the power in our substance to conceive a possible position for itself and to cast our substance with its own forces into that position. To act is to quit one's existence positioned here now, for a possible position ahead. To act is to commence, to break with what has come to pass; it is to cast what has come to be in one into the future.

The real is not simply the sum-total of all we have taken possession of and maintain present in a representation. Reality lies before us as so many possibilities of apprehension and comprehension. The possibilities we grasp are not simple diagrams held fast by our thought. The functions and potentials of things are real because they have to be reached out for by our powers, which do not possess them and may be unable to reach them. Reality is contingent; it is the eventuality of them being impossible that makes the possibilities we reach for real. The real world extends before us as a configuration of possibilities suspended in the abyss of impossibility.

Our substance acts out of a sense of the contingency of the position that supports it and out of the sense of its power to apprehend possible positions ahead and to cast itself with its own forces unto them. In every movement toward exterior things, which are grasped as nodes of possibility, we sense the contingency of the reality exposed to our initiatives and the eventuality of the impotence that things harbor. To exist in action is to cast ourselves with our own forces unto the eventuality of impotence. In every advance across the landscape which promises to support our steps toward the possibilities of vision, across its open planes and paths leading to finalities, we sense the possibility of its promises turning out to be lures, its paths turning out to be snares, and its contours harboring ambushes. It is in advancing unto the exteriority of our environment that we advance unto our death. Death is everywhere in the interstices of the world, the abyss lies behind any of its connections and beneath its paths. It is this abyss of impossibility, which shows through as we advance, that opens our understanding, indefinitely, beyond the things within reach and the ground upon which we stand, makes our stance vertiginous and without repose in itself, and makes our existence action.

To act is to give form to one's powers. One envisions possibilities open to one's powers and casts oneself unto them. One finds one's substance and recaptures one's powers in another position, and at another moment of presence; the position one reaches is real with the reality of the world. The powers with which one has left one's position take on form, which subsists in the new position as the diagram for skills. The potentials and functions of things one has taken hold of hold one's forces in forms into which one can indefinitely send again one's forces. In acting, one discovers the real possibilities of the world and finds one's forces reborn in the midst of the real potentials and functions of things. Action risks impotence, to materialize its forces.

But in finding one has acted, one also finds that one leaves something of one's powers, their very power to commence, in the inertia of forms materialized in the world which hold those forces. Something is lost—the élan of initiative which surged forth out of the energies within, the power to break with the past and to arise innocent and free, the nature of being a birth which was in every power. Something of the force one has cast forth into a possible position and figure in the world, and which is now materialized in the world, is held there as one moves on. Something of one's power of initiative is left in the rented room one painted and furnished or in the vacant lot one dug up and planted with trees and flowering shrubs last season. The giddy lightness, the soaring upsurge of force that contracted the dance step will not again be felt when one recycles that dance step as a performance. Artists cease to be artists and turn into entertainers and illustrators, simply by repeating themselves. Something of one's thought is left in the book that one has written and, were it lost, one would find one could not write the same book again. Thoughts thought all the way through no longer think anything, Merleau-Ponty said; thought illuminates only when it is not entirely clear to itself and only when it tracks forth into the unknown. The wonder with which a thought first illuminated something will not flash anew when that thought has been fixed as a truth. Something of one's ardor and wonder is left in youth and will not flame up again. Finding one's forces held in forms that one's own initiatives had actualized and feeling oneself burdened with the weight of one's own initiatives is the inner experience of aging. It is the experience of mortality, not in the active form of the power that casts itself unto the possible—possibly impotence—it conceives, but in the passing of one's powers of initiative into passivity. One does not only cast one's forces against the continuities and inertia of the world; one discharges one's forces into the inertia of the world. One does not only risk one's existence in the world, in the possibilities that turn out to be snares and ambushes, but one dies in the world and into the world. The freedom of initiative feels itself in an anxiety that is not only the apprehensiveness that senses the void of the impossible in which the possibilities ahead are suspended, but also the anxiety that is *angustia,* constriction in narrow straits, confinement in the shroud one wraps with one's own hands.

One resists this sense of inner debilitation by framing one's field of operations in such a way that each day lays out before one the tasks that one will have the strength to fulfill. One sets out to delimit one's horizons and equip one's field of operations in such a way that each day that recurs presents again an array of tasks and implements equivalent and interchangeable with those of the day that passed and the day that is coming. One casts time in the form of a succession of days that recur indefinitely, equivalent and interchangeable. One stabilizes one's practicable space in such a way that each day is full but one retains a sense of a reserve of power. In this way, one defers the day when one senses that one's powers have ebbed; one feels, after thirty years, to be as capable on the assembly-line or in the office as the twenty-year-old youth just hired. In controlling one's practicable environment, one prevents the occurrence of crises, that is, events that require all of one's resources at once and whose outcome is uncertain. One positions one's mind in an academic or industrial institution where the problems from one day to the next are equivalent and where there will never arise a problem that demands all of one's intellectual powers, before which they may prove failing. In one's free time from one's post, one mingles with others with social skills already contracted; one avoids once-in-a-lifetime encounters and adventures which one senses that one will never again have the ardor to live through. One codes and measures one's feelings so as to respond to the promises and the threats, the ceremonies and the amusements, the places and the sights, and the news and the gossip with what has been felt before and can be felt again. One shies away from the exultant or tragic eruptions, where one's heart would find itself overwhelmed or aghast, disarmed and left scarred, such that one could never again feel the same horror or tears or joy.

One takes the others as equivalent to and interchangeable with oneself. To perceive another, not simply as an object or an obstacle, but as another agency operating in the ordered world, is to put oneself potentially in his or her place. It is to perceive the other's presence as a position that one could oneself occupy and to perceive the layout about him or her as an array of paths, resources, obstacles, and snares one could manipulate if one stood there, where he or she stands. In this equivalence and interchangeability, one sees oneself in the others and sees the others in oneself.

One takes one's place in a layout of tasks another has vacated; one picks up the operations and the skills from others. One takes one's place in the library, sitting as anyone sits and recoding in one's brain the axioms and proofs of Euclid as others have done; one makes oneself a student, another student. One says what one says, what everyone and anyone says, and one invests one's own discursive powers in formulating the common truth, which does not pass when any one passes into his own final silence. One's feelings are probings and palpations whose direction and form are picked up from others and passed on to others; one feels about the news, the sights, or the music what anyone, everyone, has felt and will feel. One sees the form of a succession of days that recur indefinitely equivalent and interchangeable, and in which one has cast the time of one's life, prolonging itself in the lives of others. In this way, one gives oneself the feeling that the strength one finds again for the tasks of the day is a crest on the current of life that comes from an immemorial past and continues into the unterminating future. One blots out the sense of the loss of the ardor and wonder of initiative, with the sense of the rhythm of life-force that rises in oneself each day.

Yet anxiety trembles in this constriction of the field of operations, this confinement in the common truths, this constriction of the heart—this wisdom of experience.

The sense of void wells up in the realization that the positions and figures of oneself that one projects before oneself in action and those one has left materialized in the substance of the world, are anonymous. The postures in which one's action mobilizes one's own powers, that of a punch-press operator, a computer programmer, or an office manager, are shapes demanded of anyone by the machines, the circuitry, the layout of the industry. The forces one has as a student, factory worker, soldier, patient, or inmate are forces invested in one by the social engineering of the disciplinary archipelago, and not only the uniform one wears but the feelings and the pride one has and the instincts one obeys as parent, libertine, male or female, are variables of functions decided and maintained in the codes of gender and sexual identity. The position one occupies is a place one has taken when another, equivalent to and interchangeable with one-self, vacated it; it is a place one will leave to others. The forms one has given one's forces are configurations picked up from others and passed on to others. One touches nothing of oneself in them; one senses one has made oneself someone in making oneself anyone. One day one will not be there, and the student, lawyer, corporation executive, patient, parent, male or female one was, will be enacted by another. The positions, the performances, the gestures will not die with one; they are configurations on a wave of the current of anonymous life where birth replaces dying.

It is then that the situations and days that recur lose their urgency; one feels ineffectual and lost in the midst of tasks that have become equivalent and paths that have become interchangeable and directions reversible; the world recedes into insignificance and insubstantiality. In the foreboding sense of a day imminent in which one will not be there, there stirs an immanent anxiety that senses that the place one occupies is empty of oneself.

The anxiety finds not my own, the thought that comprehended the tasks the recurrence of the day set about me; not my own, the hands that manipulated the instruments; and not my own, the gestures that signaled to and the laughter that echoed that of the others. The anxiety suffers in the solitude of something that was not yet born in the world. It cleaves to the secret recesses where lurk powers of one's own: singular powers to know, to feel, and to give, which one's own being there engenders, which have not yet been actualized, and which will to be. One looks at one's hand, with which one can be identified, and at these dozen lines on one's finger that are found on no other of the four billion right hands in humanity, and one understands this identity and these hands have not touched what they alone can touch. One senses in the constriction of the heart a fund of force singularly one's own, a power, wired in the incomparable circuitry of one's brain, awaiting a problem in the universe for which no other brain is wired, a power in one's nervous circuitry and musculature to carve idols or to dance or to embrace as no other body can carve or dance or embrace, and a power in one's sensibility to love or to laugh or to weep as no one can. But one finds that one has not stationed oneself in the zone where these powers can find what is awaiting them and that one would have to seek in the outer deserts beyond the map of tasks that the recurrence of the days lights up for one.

Outer deserts to which I am driven by the shadow of a death coming for me. In the anxiety that trembles with the singular pulse and heat of life that feels itself and clings to itself and wills to be, there is the foreboding of an imminent moment of impossibility advancing unto it. In the paths opening to anyone, anxiety senses snares from which I shall not escape. The paths and the time of the world will continue, extending indefinitely landscapes of possibilities for others. In the imminence of impossibility that stalks my life, I see the shadow of death closing off, in the horizons of possibility that are possibilities for anyone, those that are not for me, that are for others.

To feel, in the acuteness of anxiety, the heat and the pulse of life that is singularly my own and to cling to it as a power that wills to be, is to feel the support of the ground under my feet still and to feel it supporting possibilities destined for me alone. For the anxiety with which a singular power of life is con-

cerned with itself is possible only in the conviction
that the world which made it possible harbors possibilities singularly destined for its forces. The concern
for a power wired in the incomparable circuitry of
one's brain is possible only in the conviction that a
problem in the universe, for which no other brain is
wired, awaits it; the concern for the power in one's
sensibility to love or to laugh or to weep as no one
can is possible only in the conviction that, in the back
lanes and alleys of the world, there are those who wait
for one's own kisses and caresses and there are glades
and deserts that wait for one's own laughter and tears.

The shadow of death circumscribes, in the unend-
ing array of possibilities that are possible for anyone,
what alone is possible for me. The shadow of death
stalking me in particular brings out in relief the
ground that is supporting me still and the enigmas it
harbors that are for me alone, the contours surfacing
for the tenderness of my hands alone, and the com-
panions that are there for my kisses and caresses
alone. In its dark light, anxiety finds the clairvoyance
that discerns them.

This array of possibilities open to being actualized
by the actualization of my own powers summons me,
with a summons directed by the wall of the impossible
that closes in. In responding to this imperative and
in resolutely advancing upon the possibilities that are
possible only for me, revealed by the death that is
coming for me, I recognize in the imminence of

death, not a fatality but an imperative that directs me into the figure of being that is mine alone to be. That summons my thought upon the possibilities that are for everyone and for all times, in order to disengage the possibilities that are possible singularly for me. In responding to the sense of my approaching death, I will advance unto them, discharging my forces into the possibilities the world spreads singularly before me, die into the world with my own forces. The summons that weighs on my anxiety delivers me over to the powers of an existence that is my own and into a death that is my own in the world. The fear of dying that subsists is a fear of not having the strength of patience demanded and a fear of one's lucidity and resolve not having the strength to obey the imperative of dying that summons.

It is then that one becomes aware of *others*. One no longer sees oneself in the others or sees the others in oneself. One comes to see the other in an *other place and time*. To perceive him or her as other in the midst of the equivalence and interchangeability of paths, resources, obstacles, and snares, is to see oneself bound to one's own place and tasks. It is the wall of one's own death that circumscribes the zone of possibilities that are possible for oneself and separates them from those that are for others. Another death circumscribes the expanse of possibilities that are pos-

place we may be not dying with you

sible for the other. In this deferral of his or her death in relationship to one's own, the other is different.

The mortality of the other concerns me. Not only in that it is the sense of his mortality that makes me see him as different, destined for a zone of tasks circumscribed by the death coming singularly for him. Such that, as Heidegger says, the best thing I can do for the other if I care about him is to free him for his tasks and his dying, by resolutely pursuing my own. But the tasks that are my own are projected into the world by his passage to his death. I find the shape of my own destiny in the outline of enterprises that the others traced in the world but did not have the time or the power to realize.

If the latency of impossibility suspends the substance of things in their contingent reality, it is powers of apprehension and comprehension that delineate their shape and divine their forces. The world I find under my own feet does not extend about me as a miasma in which I grope alone; I am born in a place that another has vacated and sent forth along ·paths which others have trod. For me, the world is, from the start, a field of possibilities others have apprehended and comprehended, possibilities for others. What I find as possibilities for me are possibilities others have left me. Not only possibilities which they actualized and which another too can actualize, but singular possibilities which, in actualizing their own

People other than you have shaped the world.

powers, they were not able to actualize. The one who resolved to sing his own songs found, also in the world, the singular possibilities and, in himself, the singular power to be a lover, parent, writer, adventurer, which, in setting out to sing his own songs, he had to leave to others. For to sing his own songs required all his sensibility, all his powers to grieve and to jubilate, and all his time, as to love another with a singular love requires all one's understanding and all one's heart. Gandhi, who found in himself the power to become the singular figure of a liberator and that of a saint he was born to be, left aside the power to be a statesman and a lover and a parent, which he discovered he was also born to be. In taking my place at a post others have vacated, I see in the arrangement left on things, not only the diagram of their skills that can be reinscribed on my forces, but also the outline of singular enterprises that they did not have the power to realize: possibilities they left behind, for others, for me—traces of singular imperatives. The passing of others who pursued the singular powers of their own lives speaks singularly to me.

Born in a place another vacates, summoned already by a death that is my own, apprehending the possibilities open singularly to me, I discover the others in their otherness, in the places and the possibilities that are for them. The others who pursue their own singular powers also trace out possibilities they cannot actualize and leave for me. In the handshake that recognizes our kinship, we exchange messages and resources.

In exchanging messages and resources with others, we communicate in the common time in which the insights of each are formulated in the common discourse and the forces born with each are absorbed in the anonymity of enterprises and works which endure or disintegrate in the materiality of the world. In exchanging messages and resources with the other, I sense the time opened ahead of him or her by his or her anticipation of the end; that is, the time the other extends in the world by engaging himself or herself in the field of his or her own possibilities and retaining his or her commitments. But my eyes, my touch, and my word addressed to the other divine, in the contact, the vulnerability, the weariness and the suffering, the mortality of the other. The time in which the other pursues his own tasks and approaches me is also a time of suffering and dying. There comes the time when the other can do nothing more, but has still to die. The time of his or her dying opens the black hole of a time that is not that of the common world. It is already present in the weariness and suffering that he or she has to endure alone.

In attending to the other who has to suffer and in coming to suffer with the other who is dying, one endures a time disconnected from the time of the world. Dying takes time; it extends a strange time that under-

dying

mines the time one anticipates, a time without a future, without possibilities, where there is nothing to do but endure the presence of time. What is impending is absolutely out of reach: incomprehendable, unnegatable, unconfrontable, and unpostponable. What is impending is the unknown, not even apprehendable as the impossible, as nothingness. The time of dying disconnects one's powers from ends and from their own ending. The imminence of death disconnects from one the past which one can recapture, retain, only by gathering one's forces for possibilities. One does not advance into the distance where the last moment awaits; one finds oneself suspended in a time that is drifting, in which one is constrained to go on without going anywhere. The dying takes place in an interval interminably and immemorially coming from nowhere and going nowhere, absolutely exterior to the time of a personal or interpersonal history.

A time in which there is nothing to do but suffer. A time in which you, who have come to help, can do nothing but suffer. One is held in this time outside the course of the world, by the pain. The intensity of pain does not throw one back upon one's own resources or one's potential; it backs one up against oneself, one is unable to flee and unable to retreat from oneself. Mired in oneself, one exists in the powerlessness to bear the weight of one's being. Pain does not identify the death whose imminence it senses as nothingness; pain longs for nothingness as deliverance from the dying, more strange than noth- ingness, come from within, to separate one from the exteriority of being. Pain, mired in itself, has not the force to cast itself across exteriority where one could apprehend the abyss beyond being; it is engulfed in the invasion of night and crushed by the weight of what lies in the night beyond night. One passes into passivity and dies into what comes neither as nothing- ness nor as another existence.

One suffers as one suffers, as anyone suffers, as carnal flesh suffers. One is held in a time in which one does not advance on one's own, divested of a oneself that was one's own. One dies as another, in a dying that is not one's own. One suffers, bearing the weight of passivity that invades from within, until the prostration and passivity of one's pain is exceeded by the excess of the dying that pursues its interminable course, and the one that suffers is broken and shat- tered in gasps and sobs.

seek to comfort

The hand extended to the other makes contact with the vulnerability, the weariness, and the suffering of the other and extends one into the place of the other's dying. It obeys a strange imperative. This dy- ing concerns me; one is not free to justify the death of the other, not free to justify, with the imperatives of my own tasks or those of the common work of civi- lization, leaving the dying of the other to him or her.

In the midst of objectives and equipment, the nakedness of the other's eyes seeks me out; the empty-
handedness of his gestures turn to me; the disarmed
and disarming insubstantiality of her words, which
pass without leaving a trace, single me out. His
glance, gestures, and words—importunate and insistent—disturb the order of my sphere of operations
and contest me. The other approaches across the wall
that my own death has raised about the tasks destined
for me, to contest me with her mortality.

The imperative force with which the other approaches is not in the forms his eyes outline as they
scan the landscape about me, in the forms with which
his hands inform the emptiness, or in the words he or
she formulates and which signal remote and absent
things for my understanding and my undertakings. It
lies in the surface of exposure with which he or she
faces me. His or her facing exposes the frailty and vulnerability of naked skin. It exposes the smoothness of
skin, left virginal by every expression that passes
across it and vanishes. It exposes the night of eyes,
on which, unlike the interstellar nights in which stars
extinguished millions of years ago trace their lights
still, the forms of the world leave no trace. On the
diaphanous thinness of skin with which the other is
compressed, one senses sensibility, sensitivity, and
susceptibility. One senses vulnerability and mortality
in the tremblings of pleasure that die away and the
anxieties of pain that agitate those surfaces. One

senses it in the wrinkles with which aging inscribes the pressure of imminent death. One senses it in the lassitude and torpor into which the expressions he or she addresses to me sink. One senses the other, even in presenting himself or herself in the field of equipment and resources and discharging his or her forces into the transpersonal itinerary of enterprises, sinking into the time of endurance and suffering.

The exposed surfaces of the other do not position themselves before one as so much data for one's interpretation or as so much amorphous matter for one to give form and significance to. The carnal breaks through, collapsing the distances across which its presence can be represented. Carnal surfaces expose themselves without offering possibilities to one's powers. They halt one's hands in mid-air and decline one's organization and one's projects. They afflict one with the exposedness of their discharges of pleasure and their spasms of pain, and their susceptibility. They weigh on one and deliver themselves over to one's tenderness. In the immediacy of their presence, they are irremediably exterior: the surface of a sensibility, a susceptibility, a pleasure, and a torment that is irremediably alien to one and exposes a vulnerability and an alien mortality that summons one.

One's hand, divested of its power, finds itself extending into this zone of suffering and extending its sensitivity and tenderness into this zone of an utterly alien time where nothing is offered or promised. In one's look which attends to what the other says and offers light, in one's hands clasped in acknowledgment of common tasks and commitment, and in one's words subjected to the most remote things that respond to the other, there is also contact of mortality with mortality, and accompaniment in mortality.

The touch of consolation that extends to the suffering one is not a practical force that breaks through obstacles to materialize an end. The skilled hands of the nurse and the surgeon operate on another's organism like on a machine that requires repair or a chemical compound that requires refurbishments. They anaesthetize the pain, extract the bullet, suture the torn tissues. The suffering appeals to the forbearance of the one who handles the surgical instruments and the drugs and to the compassion in his or her consoling hands. The patient convalesces in patience, enduring the time in which dying and recovering contend among themselves. The touch of consolation is not itself a medication or a protection; it is a solicitude that has no idea of what to do or how to escape. Its movement is nowise a project; one goes where one cannot go, where nothing is offered and nothing is promised. The touch of consolation is an accompaniment, by one mortal and susceptible to suffering, of the other as he sinks into the time that goes nowhere, not even into nothingness. The touch of consolation opens the path, in the time of endurance and suffer-

ing, to an accompaniment in dying and finds brotherhood with the other in the last limit of his or her destitution.

In the compassion that turns to the other, there is
fear that the other will not be able to endure and fear
that the other, mired in pain, may not be able to obey
the summons addressed to him. The other feels the
touch one brings to him as a force come from else-
where that draws him out of his pain, mired in itself,
and draws him into a suffering that depersonalizes
and that is no longer his alone, and no longer his.

One goes because one finds oneself compelled to
go; one goes so that the other not be alone in his or
her dying. Every move of one's hand that is moved
to tact and tenderness acknowledges the imperative
addressed to one in the susceptibility of the other.
One has to suffer for the others and with the others.
The grief, when the other has been taken and no
medication or comfort were possible, understands
that one has to grieve.

PHOTOGRAPHS

The photographs were taken by the author.

ALPHONSO LINGIS, Professor of Philosophy at The Pennsylvania State University, is author of *Deathbound Subjectivity, Libido: The French Existential Theories, Phenomenological Explanations*, and *Excesses: Eros and Culture*.

CPSIA information can be obtained at www.ICGtesting.com
Printed in the USA
LVOW080844260113

316853LV00008B/5/A